HC

Ir

D1245497

INEQUALITY
IN AMERICA

INEQUALITY IN AMERICA

FACTS, TRENDS, AND INTERNATIONAL PERSPECTIVES

URI DADUSH
KEMAL DERVIŞ
SARAH PURITZ MILSOM
BENNETT STANCIL

Ashland
Community & Technical College
Library

College Drive Campus

BROOKINGS INSTITUTION PRESS
Washington, D.C.

91828

Copyright © 2012
THE BROOKINGS INSTITUTION
1775 Massachusetts Avenue, N.W., Washington, D.C. 20036
www.brookings.edu

All rights reserved. No part of this publication may be reproduced or transmitted in any form or by any means without permission in writing from the Brookings Institution Press.

Library of Congress Cataloging-in-Publication data

Inequality in America : facts, trends, and international perspective /
    Uri Dadush ... [et al.].
        p. cm.
    Includes bibliographical references and index.
    ISBN 978-0-8157-2421-6 (pbk. : alk. paper)
    1. Income distribution—United States. 2. Poor—United States. 3. Wealth—United States. 4. Equality—United States. 5. United States—Economic conditions. 6. United States—Social conditions. I. Dadush, Uri B.
    HC110.I5I524 2012
    339.2'20973—dc23   2012021020

9 8 7 6 5 4 3 2 1

Printed on acid-free paper

Typeset in Sabon

Composition by Cynthia Stock
Silver Spring, Maryland

Printed by R. R. Donnelley
Harrisonburg, Virginia

CONTENTS

ACKNOWLEDGMENTS

THE AUTHORS WOULD LIKE TO express their gratitude to the many scholars and colleagues whose work on income inequality was hugely helpful in writing this book. In particular we would like to thank the participants of numerous roundtables and brainstorming sessions for their comments, including Jonathan Ostry, Michael Kumhof, Sarah Rosen Wartell, Heather Boushey, Alan Hersh, Alice Rivlin, E. J. Dionne, Nancy Birdsall, Ronald Blackwell, Homi Kharas, Matt Browne, Isabel Sawhill, Gary Burtless, and Kevin Watkins. We would also like to thank our three panelists, Branko Milanovic, Zanny Minton Beddoes, and Prakash Loungani, from the April 2012 discussion event at the Carnegie Endowment for International Peace, for their detailed comments and suggestions.

We are very fortunate to have the expert work of Larry Converse, Janet Walker, and Susan Woollen of the Brookings Institution Press, who seamlessly shepherded our book through the various stages of production, as well as Katherine Scott, who copyedited the manuscript.

And last, we thank the Carnegie Endowment for International Peace and the Brookings Institution for supporting the research underlying this book.

1 INTRODUCTION: THE CHALLENGE OF INEQUALITY

A bedrock American principle is the idea that all individuals should have the opportunity to succeed on the basis of their own effort, skill, and ingenuity.

—Federal Reserve Chairman Ben Bernanke

INCOME INEQUALITY HAS INCREASED dramatically in the United States since the late 1970s. The great economic and financial crisis that hit in 2008 and the persistent high unemployment that has come with it have drawn greater attention to the trend toward marked concentration of income at the top, little or no progress for the middle, and precariousness at the bottom of the income distribution. The problem is now squarely at the center of the political debate. Even among those who view inequality neutrally—or even positively—as the way in which markets reward performance, most agree that some of the features that accompany it, such as reduced opportunity and low social mobility, increased prevalence of poverty, and the stagnation of median household income, are undesirable. Those who traditionally are more concerned about high inequality worry that increased concentration of income is also leading to the concentration of

1

political power, which impedes efforts to mitigate inequality and even may promote policies that exacerbate it. Meanwhile, a number of economists have argued recently that the extreme concentration of income at the top may undermine macroeconomic and financial stability by making it harder to sustainably maintain strong aggregate demand or by encouraging excessive borrowing.

Our objective in this review of the challenge of inequality is to assemble in one place a readable overview of the basic facts and the issues that is accessible to both policymakers and a wider public. Our focus is squarely on the United States, but we draw on international experience and comparisons to shed light on the trends and help sketch out some possible remedies. It is also clear to us that it is impossible to separate the purely economic or technological drivers of inequality from the political processes that shape the policies influencing the distribution of income. We hope to present a comprehensive picture, tying the various dimensions of the topic together but without going into technical detail. An informed discussion of policy needs an empirical summary of the facts and of the various available interpretations. That is what we aim to provide.

Whichever of many possible measures one looks at, inequality in the United States has increased very substantially. Certainly this increased inequality seems to be part of a global trend, yet among economically advanced countries the United States is an outlier. Although it is difficult to attribute the rise in inequality to any one specific cause, it is apparent that technological change, international trade, changes in labor-market participation, the increasing role of the financial sector in the economy, the increased size of markets, and a decrease in the degree of progressivity of taxes all play some role and that several of these factors have been especially pronounced in the United States. In addition, the political environment, the loss of power of organized labor, and apparent changes in social norms affecting compensation at the top also seem to contribute to increased inequality. Though detailed policy recommendations lie beyond the scope of this book, we suggest a number of general policy orientations that could help mitigate some of the more damaging consequences of high and rising inequality, approaches that are compatible with promoting an efficient and competitive economy.

2 THE INCREASE OF INEQUALITY IN THE UNITED STATES

MEASURING INCOME INEQUALITY, EVEN in the United States, where good data are available, is complicated. Attempting to compare U.S. trends with those in other countries becomes exceedingly complicated. Precisely defining income is a challenge in and of itself. Income can be measured gross or net of taxes, including or excluding government benefits, and including or excluding realized capital gains (profits made from selling assets). Units of measurement also vary: sometimes households with multiple earners are the taxable unit and other times only individual income earners, regardless of whether or not they share a household.[1] Both official and private sources often provide data on a combination of different income measures, based on different tax units, and these different sources rarely have identical definitions of income. This poses a challenge not only when we compare across different measurements of inequality but also when we look at the same measurement of inequality calculated from different sources (see table 2-1 for a summary of how the major collectors and disseminators of data define and measure income).

---

1. To the extent more tax units live in single households, economizing on resources that they can share, the tax unit data may not reflect the real incomes involved. See Burtless (2012).

TABLE 2-1. Definitions Used to Measure Income,
by Data-Collecting Entity

Source	Earner unit	Income unit	Components of income
Congressional Budget Office	Households	Real income, adjusted to reflect U.S. consumer price index inflation	Market income: Labor income (wages and salaries, including employer contributions to health insurance, Social Security, etc.), business income, realized capital gains, capital income excluding capital gains, and other income sources, including retirement income for past services.
			Post-tax and transfer income: Market income plus government transfers, including Social Security cash payments, unemployment insurance, veterans' benefits, Food Stamps, Medicare, and Medicaid, CHIP, minus federal taxes (income, payroll, social insurance, and corporate).
U.S. Census Bureau	Households	Real income, adjusted by U.S. consumer price index	Income received on a regular basis, including earnings, Social Security, unemployment compensation and veterans' benefits. Excludes capital gains and noncash transfers (Food Stamps and health benefits). Measures income before payment of income, Social Security, Medicare, and other taxes.
World Top Incomes Database	Tax units (single adult or married couple filing jointly)	Real income, adjusted by U.S. consumer price index	Income from salaries and wages, business income, dividends, interest, rents, and other small sources of income. Realized capital gains are included in a separate series. Measures income before payment of individual income and payroll taxes but after payment of employers' payroll and corporate taxes. Excludes government transfer payments (usually less than 1 percent of total income).
OECD	Households	Real income, adjusted to reflect consumer price indices	Disposable income. Measures income after taxes and government cash transfers.

Source: Authors' compilation and CBO (2011).

There are many ways to look at the distribution of income within the population, but we will focus our attention on three common measurements: the Gini index, the broadest measure of inequality; the comparison of median income versus the nation's average, or mean, household income; and the share of incomes at the very top and bottom of the distribution relative to the rest of the distribution. These indicators measure inequality at a point in time. We also discuss social mobility: how those born at the low end of the income distribution tend to fare over time compared to those born in the middle or at the top of the distribution. Low social mobility can be a sign that there is inequality of opportunity, implying that the economy's human capital or talent is not optimally deployed.

Broad Inequality

The most widely used measure of overall inequality is the Gini index, also called the Gini concentration ratio and the Gini coefficient, which is calculated to indicate the relationship between shares of income and shares of the population. Gini values range from zero (perfect equality) to 1 (perfect inequality, hypothetical values that are never reached).[2] The greater the Gini coefficient, the greater is the concentration of income and the more unequal the distribution of income.

A recent Congressional Budget Office (CBO) report on household income inequality found that the U.S. Gini index rose from 0.48 in 1979 to 0.59 in 2007.[3] Evidence of this trend, and its continuation through 2010, is also found in data provided by the U.S. Census Bureau.[4] After hovering around 0.40 throughout the

2. Theoretically the Gini coefficient can range from 0 to 1, but in practice values fall within a narrower range, from about 0.25 to 0.65.

3. The CBO compares 1979 and 2007 (rather than through 2010) because these two years were similar in terms of economic activity—both experienced economic peaks just prior to recession (Congressional Budget Office 2011, p. 9).

4. The Census Bureau's definition of income includes pre-tax market income plus government benefits such as Social Security income payments, unemployment insurance, and veteran's benefits, but does not include capital gains—which *is* included

1970s, the Gini index as reported by the Census Bureau rose from 0.46 in 2007 to 0.47 in 2010. (Note that these measures are smaller than those reported by the CBO, resulting from differences in the definitions of income used to calculate the index; see table 2-1.)[5] Importantly, the CBO data are based on market income—income before taxes and transfers—whereas census data do include some government transfers. Measures that do not include taxes and government transfers overstate inequality in terms of capacity to spend, since government taxes and transfers typically redistribute income downward. Indeed, historically, taxes and transfers have reduced the magnitude of inequality in the United States, though at a decreasing rate over time. These policies have done little, if anything, to slow the increase in inequality: the CBO estimates that in 2007, federal transfers and taxes decreased the Gini coefficient by about 17 percent. By way of comparison, the redistributive effect in 1979 was greater, with a 23 percent reduction in the Gini. Thus, although taxes and transfers have a redistributive effect, the extent of redistribution has weakened over time, implying that over the last three decades changes in government policies have worked in the same direction as market forces, toward greater inequality. The U.S. Gini index for disposable income (income after federal transfers and taxes), as calculated by the CBO, has continued to rise, going from 0.37 to 0.49 between 1979 and 2007.[6]

Rising inequality is by no means unique to the United States. Seventeen of the twenty-two OECD (Organization for Economic Cooperation and Development) countries for which data are available have seen inequality rise from the mid-1980s to the late 2000s, as measured by the household Gini coefficient. In

in the CBO definition. See U.S. Census Bureau, "How the Census Bureau Measures Poverty," 2011 (www.census.gov/hhes/www/poverty/about/overview/measure.html).

5. See U.S. Census Bureau Historical Tables, 2010 (www.census.gov/hhes/www/income/data/historical/inequality).

6. Note that these numbers differ from the Census Bureau Gini measurements reported earlier, owing to differences in measurement of income. See note 3 for more details.

fact, only two of these countries, Turkey and Greece, have seen a decline in their Gini coefficients (see figure 2-1).[7]

Nevertheless, among developed countries the United States stands out. Relative to the countries examined by the OECD, the U.S. Gini index in the mid-1980s was second highest, behind Mexico, and this remained true through the mid-2000s. Mexico is classified as a developing country by the World Bank, which found income distribution in developing countries be more unequal than in advanced countries, so the statistical proximity of the United States to Mexico is startling, to say the least.

The Man in the Street

The nation's average income is not an accurate portrayal of the typical household. This is because the income distribution is not symmetrical: there are many more people who earn lower incomes than rich people who earn high incomes. The median income gives a better picture of the true typical household income in the United States; it is the income level at which half of all households earn more and half of all households earn less. The CBO calculates that the average, or mean, market income in 2007 was $64,500, whereas the median income was much lower, $41,700. The real median household income after taxes and transfers (adjusted for inflation) increased by 35 percent between 1979 and 2007, whereas the average household income saw a 62 percent increase in those years. This growing gap between the average and median incomes indicates a pattern in which income growth was heavily weighted toward households with income well above the median income levels (see figure 2-2).

Looking at the median and mean household income before federal transfers and taxes—which are redistributive effects, albeit

7. See Organization for Economic Cooperation and Development (2011a). It is almost certain that future data will show that the Greek crisis led to much worse inequality also in Greece.

FIGURE 2-1. Income Distribution in Twenty-Two OECD Countries
as Measured by the Gini Coefficient

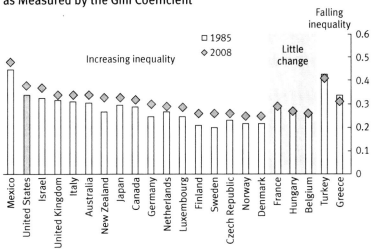

Source: Organization for Economic Cooperation and Development (2011a).

less so—shows, as expected, an even wider gap (see figure 2-2): the average real household market income grew by 58 percent between 1979 and 2007, whereas the median real household income increased by a meager 19 percent over almost forty years. This reflects the fact that household market incomes have become more concentrated, and at an increasing rate.

Crucially, the figure also shows that the median household saw a decline in real income during the early 2000s and there has been little growth over the whole last decade. Alan Krueger, the chairman of the White House Council of Economic Advisers, recently estimated that if, in the early 2000s, real median household market income had grown at the same rate as it did in the 1990s, middle-class households would have about $8,900 more to spend per year than they currently do.[8]

8. See Krueger (2012).

FIGURE 2-2. Cumulative Growth in Average and Median Household Income after Taxes and Transfers

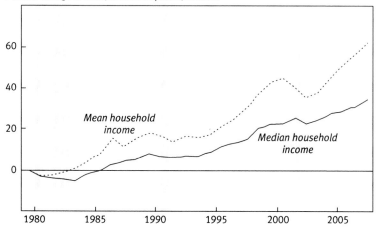

Percent change in real (inflation-adjusted) income

Source: Congressional Budget Office (2011, p. 2).

The Gini coefficient, the mean household income, and the median household income are useful measures for showing an overall trend in the income distribution, and they show that it is undeniably becoming more concentrated. However, these measurements are somewhat insensitive to changes within portions of the income distribution. For example, a relatively small absolute decline in the incomes of those at the lower end of the income distribution may have a big impact on their living standards but will only be reflected in a small change in the Gini.[9] It is useful, therefore, to look more directly at how particular shares of income within the distribution have behaved.

9. See Radelet and others (2001, pp. 120–25) for a more in-depth discussion of methods for measuring inequality.

FIGURE 2-3. Cumulative Growth in Mean and Median Household
Market Income

Percent change in real (inflation-adjusted) income since 1979

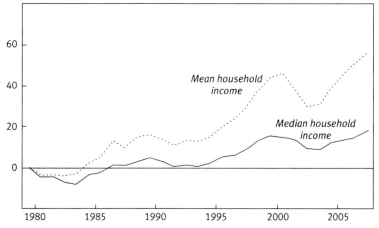

Source: Congressional Budget Office (2011, p. 6).

Income at the Extremes

The ratios of top-quintile incomes to bottom-quintile incomes
reveal that overall inequality not only has increased in the
United States but also has become particularly pronounced at
the extremes. The growing gulf between the rich and the poor
is the result of remarkable gains at the very top of the income
distribution and little advance at the bottom. Within the top
quintile—the top 20 percent of earners—the income of the top
1 percent of earners has soared. The CBO finds that market
income share of the top 1 percent of households doubled, from
around 10 percent of the total market income in the 1970s to
more than 20 percent in 2012. Meanwhile, incomes of the 80th-
through 99th-percentile households remaining in the top quintile saw their share of income fall. This explosion at the very

top has had a strong effect on both the level and growth of overall income inequality, particularly since 1980. According to CBO estimates, from 1979 to 2007, excluding the top 1 percent would have resulted in a 13.8 percent increase in market income inequality as measured by the Gini coefficient, compared to the actual overall increase of 23.2 percent.[10]

Historical studies estimate that this degree of income concentration has not been seen since the days before the Great Depression. According to the World Top Incomes Database, which is created using income tax records for twenty-two countries, the top 1 percent of U.S. tax filers, individuals or couples filing one return, earned 20 percent of U.S. market income in 2010.[11] This share was down from 23.5 percent in 2007, reflecting the losses from the financial crisis, but was still a share not seen since 1928. The top 0.01 percent of tax units—about 15,000 units of over 150 million—earned 5 percent of the total income. Before the financial crisis this group's share exceeded 6 percent, the highest on record. If the income distribution were perfectly equal, the income of these 15,000 tax units would have equaled that of over 9 million tax units.

The ratios discussed thus far include income from realized capital gains, which is the most unequally distributed source of income (see the later section, "Income Channels and Inequality"). Even excluding capital gains, however, the World Top Incomes Database shows that the current level of income concentration at the top has not been reached since 1929 (see figure 2-4).

This rapid growth of incomes at the top is in contrast with little or negative growth at the bottom of the distribution. The Census

10. Note that the difference in these Gini coefficients is due to measurement differences across sources, one coming from the Census Bureau and the other from the Congressional Budget Office.

11. See Alvaredo and others, "World Top Incomes Database" (http://g-mond. parisschoolofeconomics.eu/topincomes).The database provides data including and excluding capital gains. Unless otherwise noted, references to this source include capital gains.

FIGURE 2-4. Market Income Share of the Top 1 Percent, 1913–2010

Percent share

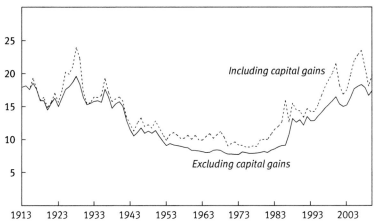

Source: Alvaredo and others, "World Top Incomes Data Base."

Bureau estimates that from 1979 to 2010, the real household income of the bottom 10 percent grew by only 3.6 percent over three decades—a negligible amount.[12] Though these details vary from study to study, depending on how income and tax units are defined, the conclusion is inescapable: income growth at the bottom of the distribution has been slow and has been far outpaced by that at the top.[13]

International comparisons confirm that these phenomena have been particularly pronounced in the United States. Of all countries

12. See U.S. Census Bureau, Selected Measures of Household Income Dispersion: 1967 to 2010," table A-3 (www.census.gov/hhes/www/income/data/.../inequality/taba2.pdf).

13. The inclusion of all medical benefits received by low-income groups moderates the inequality between the lower and middle deciles. From a philosophical and ethical point of view, it can be argued, however, that medical expenditures that compensate for the costs of a medical condition beyond an individual's control are of a different nature than other transfer payments.

in the World Top Incomes Database, the United States is home to the highest income shares for the top 1, top 0.1 and top 0.01 percent of earners.[14] Only South Africa and Argentina, two developing countries marked by long histories of deep inequality and social divisions, even come close to the U.S. figures.

Among major developed countries, the United States stands out in another respect: over the four decades since 1970, the extraordinary fact is that there has been almost no increase in average incomes among the bottom 90 percent of earners. From 1970 to 2007 (that is, pre-crisis), average real incomes, excluding capital gains, only increased by about 5 percent, yet for the years 1970 through 2010 (post-crisis), the average actually decreased by 6 percent. By contrast, in Australia, Canada, France, Italy, New Zealand, Norway, and Sweden, the average income of the bottom 90 percent of earners grew on average by more than 60 percent over roughly the same period (see figure 2-5). Note that this figure seems to contradict the very slow but positive growth of median incomes reported by the CBO.[15] There are several plausible explanations for this discrepancy. As can be seen in table 2-1, the definitions of income vary by source. It is important to reiterate that the World Top Incomes Database reports data by tax unit, not by household. A single tax unit includes couples filing jointly, with dependents, or individuals filing separately, with dependents. For this reason data collected by tax unit should not be expected to match data collected by household,

14. Countries in the World Top Incomes Database with data through at least 2000 are Argentina, Australia, Canada, China, Denmark, Finland, France, Indonesia, Ireland, Italy, Japan, Mauritius, New Zealand, Norway, Portugal, Singapore, South Africa, Spain, Sweden, the United Kingdom, and the United States. These U.S. income-share figures exclude income from capital gains because income shares including capital gains are only available for a few countries. See Alvaredo and others, "World Top Incomes Database."

15. See U.S. Census Bureau, Selected Measures of Household Income Dispersion: 1967 to 2010," table A-3 (www.census.gov/hhes/www/income/data/.../inequality/taba2.pdf), p. 4.

FIGURE 2-5. Average Percentage of Real Income Growth in the
Bottom 90 Percent of Earners, 1970–2005[a]

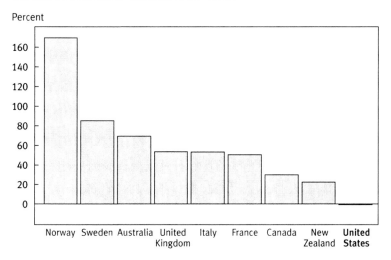

Percent

Source: Alvaredo and others, "World Top Incomes Data Base."
a. Countries with data at least through 2000 but varies due to data availability; capital gains excluded due to lack of data.

as is the case for data collected by the CBO and OECD and for many census studies.[16]

Unsurprisingly, the slow growth at the bottom and rapid growth at the top have polarized the extremes of the income distribution more in the United States than in any other advanced country. Despite some holes in the data, it can be confidently asserted that the U.S. ratios of top-quintile and top-decile incomes to bottom-quintile and bottom-decile incomes are the highest in the OECD. That is, the ratio of the top 20 percent to the bottom 20 percent is higher in the U.S. than in any other OECD country.

16. In addition, as is discussed in more detail in the demographics section, the changing composition of U.S. households likely amplifies the differences between tax unit and household data. For example, women typically earn lower incomes than men, so as women enter the workforce, average incomes, ceteris paribus, would fall while household incomes would likely rise.

The same is true for the top 10 percent and the bottom 10 percent. All measures of income inequality in the United States point to the same conclusion: inequality is rising and reaching levels not seen since before the Great Depression of the 1930s, and it is the very large concentrations at the top of the income distribution that are driving this increase. The income gap between the top and the rest began to widen at the beginning of the late 1970s, and this trend has continued, after a brief pause following the 2008 financial crisis. Data for 2011 and 2012 are not yet available, but we guess that the figures will show that inequality in 2011 and 2012, measured by the various definitions used here, will have increased again and will be close to or higher than the level it had reached in 2007. This is because capital and business income and income derived from capital gains will have risen, while real wages will hardly have increased and in many cases will have decreased.[17] About two decades ago, the country's very highest earners began to dramatically outpace the rest in the rate of their income advances. Many other developed countries have seen the income distribution become more unequal, but the divergence in the United States has been the most dramatic, especially in the extent to which the divergence stems from the concentration of income at the top.

Income Sources and Inequality

Examining the sources of income—labor and capital—sheds some light on the proximate causes of widening inequality (a discussion of the deeper causes of increased inequality will follow in chapter 4). Some individuals receive more of their income from labor while others receive more of their income from returns on capital. Income

17. Capital income (excluding capital gains) comprises taxable and tax-exempt interest, dividends paid by corporations (but not dividends from S corporations, which are considered part of business income), positive rental income, and corporate income taxes. Capital gains are considered separately and not included in this measure of capital income.

FIGURE 2-6. Income Concentration Index, by Major Source of Income

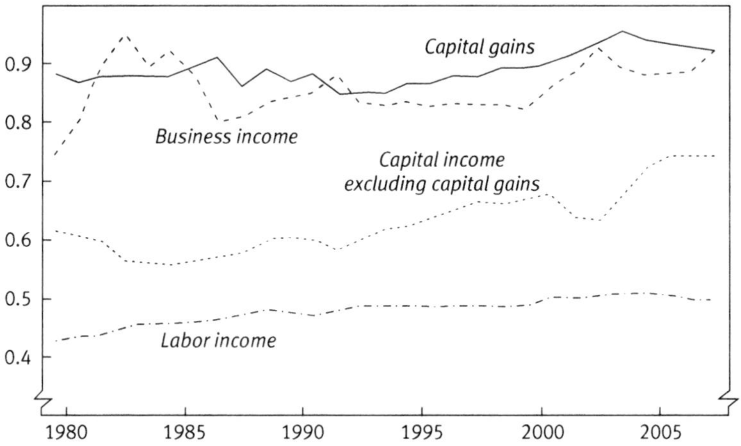

Source: Congressional Budget Office (2011).

can become more unequal either because labor or capital incomes become more concentrated or because capital income, which tends to be more concentrated, becomes a more important source of total income. As it turns out, both of these factors were at play in the United States: the CBO estimates that changes in concentration by source account for nearly 80 percent of the increase in the Gini coefficient for market income between 1979 and 2007, and shifts from less- to more-concentrated sources account for the remaining 20 percent. The CBO calculated concentration indices for each major income source (see figure 2-6), where greater concentration values, measured on the vertical axis, signify greater income inequality. The graph shows that although labor income has become more unequal (concentrated) since 1979, it is still much less concentrated than the other sources of income, most notably capital gains.[18] To put

18. Capital gains is defined as profits realized from the sale of assets. Increases in the value of assets prior to their sale are not considered "realized" and thus are not included in market income.

this in perspective, in 1979 the bottom 80 percent of the population received 60 percent of total labor income and 41 percent of total capital income.[19] By 2007, the bottom 80 percent received just under 50 percent of labor income and only 25 percent of capital income.[20] Thus, the bottom four quintiles of the income distribution saw a reduction in their share of both labor and capital income.

That all sources of income have grown more unequal explains, at least in part, the increase in income inequality in the United States. In addition, the second dimension—the composition of total income—also helps to explain growing inequality. The pie charts in figure 2-7 show that the share of labor income in total market income has decreased by approximately eight percentage points over the past twenty-eight years, whereas the share of income from capital gains, capital income, and business income have together increased by five percentage points. Other income, which includes income received in retirement for past services, makes up the remaining three percentage points.[21] This shift is important—the data show that over time the income channels that are less equal are making up a greater part of total market income.

Social Mobility: How Individuals Fare over Time

Most Americans have long believed that they have equal opportunity to achieve and succeed by dint of their own efforts. A Pew Charitable Trust survey published in 2011 reports that 68 percent of Americans still believe they are in control of their own economic situation and that they have achieved or will achieve the American Dream.[22] A 2011 Gallup poll finds that 70 percent of

19. Included in this calculation is income from capital gains, capital income (other capital income such as taxable and tax-exempt interest, dividends, rental income and corporate income taxes), and business income.

20. Congressional Budget Office (2011).

21. The CBO defines "other income" as including all other sources of income not measured as labor, capital gains, capital income, or business income.

22. See Pew Charitable Trusts, Economic Mobility Project (2011).

FIGURE 2-7. Comparison of 1979 and 2007 Share of Pre-Tax Market Income, by Income Source

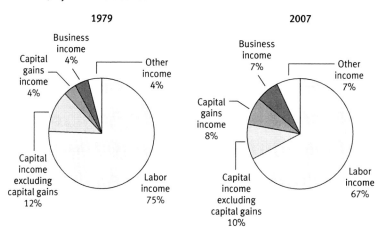

Source: Congressional Budget Office (2011).

Americans believe that increasing equality of opportunity should be an important or very important task for the federal government. The poll also reports that the percentage who feel that there is not much opportunity has gone up from 17 percent in 1998 to 41 percent in 2011.[23] Income inequality has undoubtedly increased over the last four decades, but has *opportunity* in America changed as well?

Measuring income mobility is more complicated than measuring income inequality. Income mobility has a time dimension—mobility can occur over a short period of time, over a lifetime, or between generations. The following questions are commonly asked to try to measure income mobility and opportunity:

23. Gallup, "Americans Prioritize Economy over Reducing the Wealth Gap," December 16, 2011 (www.gallup.com/poll/151568/americans-prioritize-growing-economy-reducing-wealth-gap.aspx?version=print).

—Do children achieve higher living standards than their parents?

—Do children of poor families often catch up with the children of rich families?

—Is there intergenerational mobility or do poor families remain poor and rich families, rich?

These kinds of questions are important. As a result of economic growth, all children may be better off than their parents, but children born in poor families may still remain relatively poor.

A 2007 study, the Economic Mobility Project, undertaken jointly by the Pew Charitable Trust and the Brookings Institution, estimates that 40 percent of children born to parents in the bottom quintile of the income distribution will remain there—and 60 percent of the children will move up.[24] At first glance this may seem like a reasonable number, but the data also suggest that this 60 percent may not move far above the lowest quintile. The report estimates that 23 percent of children born into the bottom quintile will move up to the lower-middle quintile and 19 percent will move up to the middle quintile. A 2006 Center for American Progress (CAP) report estimates that children born into families with income in the bottom 20 percent of the income distribution have just a 1 percent chance of reaching the top 5 percent of the income distribution, whereas a child born into a rich family (defined as the top 5 percent of the family income distribution) has a 22 percent chance of remaining in the top 5 percent as an adult. In short, a child's economic opportunity is highly influenced by his or her parents' economic position (see figure 2-8).[25] Additionally, disaggregating U.S. mobility data by race shows that big differences persist. A study by the Economic Policy Institute estimates that white workers are ten times as likely as African American workers to make it into the top 25 percent of the income distribution.

24. See Isaacs, Sawhill, and Haskins (2008).
25. Hertz (2006). See also Sawhill (2012).

FIGURE 2-8. Where Kids End Up on the Income Ladder as Adults

Percentage ending up in each fifth

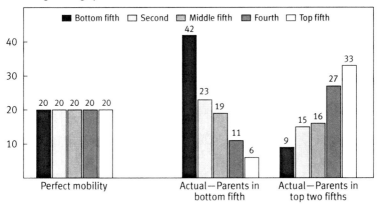

Source: Isaacs, Sawhill, and Haskins (2008).

Another important dimension of economic mobility in the United States is relative intragenerational mobility: How does an individual's income change within his or her generation relative to his or her peers' income changes? A 2007 report by the U.S. Treasury Department found that there is "considerable" short-term mobility. The study reviewed a sample of individuals' taxpayer data between 1996 and 2005 and found that "close to half of all taxpayers moved from the bottom quintile to a higher income quintile during the period."[26] But as with intergenerational mobility, one must be cognizant of the trend that those who begin at the bottom of the distribution are much more likely to stay near the bottom. Moving up one quintile from the bottom does not necessarily represent the level of upward mobility that serves as the foundation for the American Dream; but one need not travel

26. U.S. Department of the Treasury, "Income Mobility in the U.S. from 1996 to 2005," 2007 (www.treasury.gov/resource.../incomemobilitystudy 03-08revise.pdf).

far up the income distribution for the movement to be interpreted that way. It is also critical to keep in mind that measures of mobility are extremely sensitive to the population measured. For example, including sixteen-year-olds may paint a very different picture than starting at the age of twenty-two, because sixteen-year-olds typically earn small part-time wages, so the increase to a full-time job (particularly after college) artificially inflates wage increases, and therefore mobility.

The 2007 Treasury Department report on mobility also found that only 25 percent of the earners who in 1996 were in the top .01 percent remained in that income group in 2005. This reinforced other studies' findings that suggested that in a given year, income among the very rich reflects windfalls. These studies show that there is high mobility at the very top of the income distribution; in the bottom fifth, however, earners lack mobility.

Distinguishing between absolute mobility (how children fare relative to their parents in terms of absolute real income) and relative mobility (how children born into poor and wealthy families fare relative to one another) is crucial when thinking about the appropriate policy response. Increasing absolute mobility requires policies that raise economic growth, whereas affecting relative mobility requires policies that affect the distribution of opportunities across income classes.

How does America's mobility compare with that of other countries? Figure 2-9 compares earnings mobility of various developed countries. On the horizontal axis the earnings ability is expressed from the intergenerational earnings elasticity between fathers and sons as calculated by the OECD.[27] The vertical axis measures income inequality as expressed by the Gini coefficient.[28] Earnings

---

27. Organization for Economic Cooperation and Development (2011a).

28. It is more common to compare earnings mobility between fathers and sons because it is more difficult to determine work patterns for women as a result of changes in social attitudes between generations.

FIGURE 2-9. Earnings Mobility (2007) and Income Inequality,
About 2005[a]

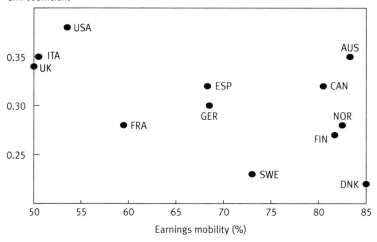

Gini coefficient

Earnings mobility (%)

Source: Organization for Economic Cooperation and Development (2011a).
a. Countries with data through 2000 but varies due to data availability.

mobility of zero percent means that sons earn the same as their
fathers; 100 percent would mean that there is no relationship
between the earnings of fathers and their sons. At 50 percent,
the United States' earnings mobility is on the low end compared
to European countries; some of which have earnings mobility as
high as 80 percent. In other words, compared to international
data, a parent's income in the United States is relatively more
predictive of incomes for his or her children than in other developed countries. The figure also suggests that countries with higher
inequality tend to have lower intergenerational mobility.

Is high inequality itself a major cause of low mobility? In their
influential book, *The Spirit Level: Why More Equal Societies
Almost Always Do Better*, Richard G. Wilkinson and Kate Pickett
argue that inequality in developed countries is the cause of wor-
risome trends across a range of social indicators, including crime,

FIGURE 2-10. Inequality and Education Outcomes:
Average of Math, Science, and Reading Scores in OECD 2009 PISA
(Program for International Student Assessment)

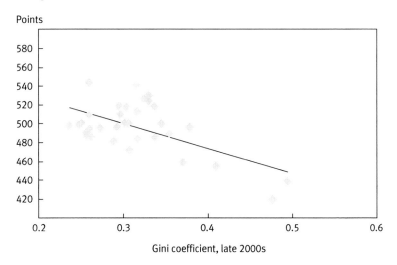

Points

Gini coefficient, late 2000s

Source: Organization for Economic Cooperation and Development (2009).

physical and mental health, teenage pregnancies, and trust.[29] They
find a negative correlation between inequality and education outcomes (OECD data are similar; see figure 2-10), suggesting that
high inequality can become self-reinforcing. Wilkinson and Pickett's arguments are based on a survey of indicators and studies
rather than on a statistical analysis that controls rigorously for
multiple factors, and they by no means close the debate on the
social effects of income inequality, but they nevertheless present a
highly suggestive case that high inequality has numerous undesirable consequences, including those that affect the prospects for
upward mobility.

29. Wilkinson and Pickett (2010).

3 THREE OTHER WORRYING TRENDS ASSOCIATED WITH RISING INEQUALITY

THERE ARE AT LEAST three disturbing trends associated with the recent American experience—the increased prevalence of poverty, increased macroeconomic instability, and the potentially wasteful and increasing expenditure on "positional goods," goods from which consumers derive utility based on their consumption relative to that of others, rather than from the goods themselves. We believe that these trends are associated with rising inequality, in the sense that they are partly a result of increased inequality or that other underlying forces account for increased inequality as well as increased poverty, increased macroeconomic instability, and the increased prominence of positional goods. In the case of poverty, the role of inequality is relatively obvious. In that of macroeconomic instability the association with inequality is more controversial. The increased prevalence of positional goods appears to result from increased inequality and in turn spurs a vicious cycle of ever-greater income inequality.

Increased Poverty

No discussion of the U.S. income distribution can ignore those at the very bottom—a group whose growth in size in recent years is troubling. The U.S. Census Bureau defines the poverty rate as the proportion of people who are below an income threshold that varies by family size and composition. If a family's total income is below the threshold, then that family and every individual in it is considered to be in poverty.[1] The United States' official annual poverty rate, 15.1 percent, is at its highest level since 1993. The financial crisis has been particularly painful: since 2007, the poverty rate has risen by almost three percentage points, pushing 8.8 million more people below the poverty line. But poverty was already increasing before the recession.

Especially disturbing is that poverty rates are very high among children and minorities. Twenty-two percent of people under eighteen and 25.3 percent of children under seven are poor, compared to average rates of 18.7 percent and 20.7 percent, respectively, for these groups over the last forty years. Black and Hispanic poverty rates, though close to or below historic averages, are still staggeringly high, around 27 percent, and 35 to 40 percent of black and Hispanic children under eighteen are poor. Poverty in metropolitan areas, at 14.9 percent, is at its highest level since 1960.

During the period from 1975 to 2010, the population group whose income was less than 50 percent of the poverty line grew far faster than any other population group (see figure 3-1). Indeed, over the past thirty-five years, the poorer the group, the faster the population belonging to that group has grown.

As figure 3-1 shows, the distribution among those who are poor or nearly poor appears to be becoming more unequal. The data also show that the increase in poverty has been greatest for working-age individuals, consistent with the fact that incomes at the low end have stagnated and unemployment has increased (see figure 3-2). The poverty rate for people age eighteen to sixty-four, 13.7 percent, is at its highest level on record—records go back to 1966. Since 1966, the number of working-age people living in poverty

---

1. U.S. Census Bureau, "How the Census Bureau Measures Poverty," 2011 (www.census.gov/hhes/www/poverty/about/overview/measure.html).

FIGURE 3-1. Growth of Population by Ratio of Income to the Poverty Line, 1975–2010

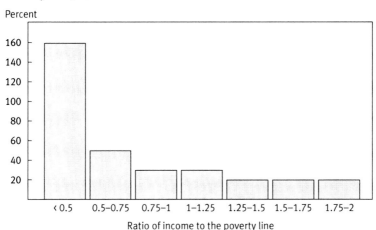

Source: Authors' calculations, based on U. S. Census Bureau, Historical Poverty Tables, "Table 5. Percent of People by Ratio of Income to Poverty Level" (www.census.gov/hhes/www/poverty/data/ historical/people.html).

has more than doubled, from 11 million to 26 million. By contrast, the number of elderly in poverty has fallen, from 5.1 to 3.5 million, even though the elderly population has more than doubled in size, to 39 million. The poverty rate for children has fluctuated during this period, but over 95 percent of children living in poverty are members of families that are already living in poverty.

The share of workers (people actually employed) living in poverty is also high. In 2010, 7 percent of workers were poor, a larger proportion than in any year since 1987 except in the years from 1992 to 1994. Yet two thirds of poor people were unemployed for all of 2010, the highest percentage since 1987, suggesting that the rise in poverty has been primarily the result of unemployment rather than a drop in relative wages of the poor employed. How does the situation in the United States compare with the poverty rate and inequality in other advanced countries? Since the 1980s,

FIGURE 3-2. Poverty Rate by Age

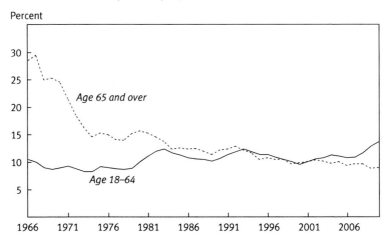

Source: U.S. Census Bureau, "How the Census Bureau Measures Poverty" (www.census.gov/hhes/
www/poverty/about/overview/measure.html).

the U.S. poverty rate (defined for international comparisons as
the percentage of households earning less than 50 percent of the
median income) was close to the OECD average, before accounting
for taxes and transfers. But after accounting for taxes and transfers, poverty rates in the United States have been among the highest in the OECD—17.3 percent by the late 2000s, higher than any
other OECD country except Israel and 150 percent of the group
average. Even after accounting for public services such as social
safety net policies like unemployment benefits, poverty rates in the
United States are the highest in the OECD, which includes several
middle-income developing countries such as Mexico and Turkey.[2]

2. See Organization for Economic Cooperation and Development (2011b).
The OECD includes the monetary value of public services in its category called
"extended income." In 2007 the extended-income poverty rate—defined as the
percentage of households earning less than 50 percent of the median extended
income—was 10.3 percent in the United States. By contrast, the average OECD
extended income poverty rate was 5.5 percent.

FIGURE 3-3. Change in Poverty and Inequality in OECD Countries, Mid-1990s–2010[a]

Percent

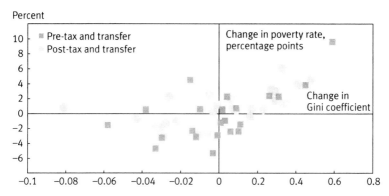

Source: OECD, "Dataset: Income Distribution and Poverty Income Distribution—Poverty," data extracted on December 5, 2011, 20:57 UTC (GMT) from OECD.Stat.

a. Data availability varies by country, and not all points represent 2010.

Increased income inequality and the rise in poverty as defined in these studies are clearly associated. Various studies and direct international comparisons provide support for the link between rising inequality and increased poverty. A study by two Federal Reserve economists, Mary Daly and Robert Valetta, found that the dispersion of men's wages has had a substantial impact on increasing poverty, and an OECD study found, not surprisingly, that poverty and inequality tend to move in unison.[3] Figure 3-3 shows a statistically significant correlation between the changes in Gini coefficients, both pre- and post-tax, and government transfers, and in the corresponding poverty rate for OECD countries since 1995.

Because the OECD defines poverty in relative terms—households earning less than 50 percent of the median income—the relationship between poverty and inequality is partly mechanical:

3. See Daly and Valletta (2004); Organization for Economic Cooperation and Development (2011a).

as the income distribution becomes more dispersed, a larger portion of the population will be below the poverty line, even if all incomes are rising. In contrast to the OECD, the U.S. Census measure of poverty sets the poverty threshold relative not to what others earn but to the cost of basic nutritional requirements. Though the poverty threshold is frequently adjusted for inflation, official poverty thresholds are not adjusted for increases in the costs of standard of living. Therefore, the U.S. measure is more absolute than relative.[4] The U.S. poverty threshold has fallen from about 50 percent of the median income in 1960 to about 30 percent of the median income in 2010.

This "relatively absolute" measure of poverty differs from those typically used for developing countries; these measures draw the poverty line at incomes of less than $1.25 or $2.00 per day, adjusted for purchasing power. Such measures would be useless if applied to advanced countries because of the relative prosperity of even the poorest Americans compared to most of the world. For example, adjusting for purchasing power, Branko Milanovic finds that households in the 15th percentile of the income scale in the United States—roughly those at the poverty line—are at around the 85th percentile globally (adjusting for purchasing power).[5] But this kind of international comparison can be misleading, in part because it is difficult to capture in one index such as the purchasing power parity (PPP) exchange rate the huge differences in prices and consumption baskets across countries of vastly different incomes and preferences.

In any event, relative poverty matters. As is noted in a U.S. Government Accountability Office report, "Poverty in America: Economic Research Shows Adverse Impacts on Health Status

4. For an overview of the current U.S. poverty measure and suggested improvements to the measuring method, see Short (2011); for a history of the measure, see Fisher (1997).

5. Milanovic (2011).

and Other Social Conditions as Well as the Economic Growth Rate," in the United States, "lower-income individuals experience higher rates of chronic illness, disease, and disabilities, and also die younger than those who have higher incomes."[6] By some accounts, the life expectancy of the poor is just 75 percent that of higher-income individuals, in part because many lack health insurance, and health care in the United States is expensive. More than 30 percent of poor individuals in the United States were not covered by health insurance for all of 2010, more than twice the rate of the non-poor. This is in contrast with other OECD countries (excluding Turkey and Mexico), which "have now achieved close to universal coverage of the population for a core set of health services."[7] The GAO report continues, "Regardless of whether poverty is a cause or an effect, the conditions associated with poverty limit the ability of low-income individuals to develop the skills, abilities, knowledge, and habits necessary to fully participate in the labor force." Finally, a small, though far from insignificant, share of poor adults in the United States report sometimes being hungry. According to a report by the Heritage Foundation, "Air Conditioning, Cable TV, and an Xbox: What Is Poverty in the United States Today?" in the early 2000s, 7.4 percent of poor households reported sometimes or often not having enough food; if this percentage persists (as one would expect, given what we know about poverty trends), about 3.5 million Americans will go without sufficient food for part of this year.[8]

Macroeconomic Instability

New arguments are emerging that high and rising levels of inequality may be a cause of increased macroeconomic instability because they contribute to a fraying of the political consensus,

6. U.S. Government Accountability Office (2007, p. 9).
7. Organization for Economic Cooperation and Development (2010).
8. Rector and Sheffield (2011).

are associated with boom-bust credit cycles, and may lead to a chronic weakness of effective demand. For a long time few economists, even those concerned about inequality, thought about it in the context of macroeconomic policy. There was a time, early in the twentieth century, when some believed that capitalism would be vulnerable because of a tendency toward a chronic lack of sufficient aggregate demand due to increases in income concentration at the top. But as income distribution improved after the 1930s and macroeconomic policy became a more powerful tool for stabilizing economic conditions, these concerns practically disappeared. Now they are reemerging.

Confirming views long held by economists, raw survey data and some econometric studies indicate that savings rates rise considerably as incomes rise, and also that savings rates at the bottom of the income distribution are likely to be negative.[9] As income shares diverge—and particularly if middle and low incomes stagnate, as they have in the United States—those left behind borrow to maintain their absolute (and possibly relative) consumption levels, especially if credit is freely available. This can lead to an unsustainable increase in debt; as leverage rises, debt levels eventually reach a tipping point, as happened in the United States in 1929 and 2007. Such scenarios, which also include a widening current account deficit, are outlined in a model of the economy developed by Michael Kumhof and Romain Ranciere.[10]

A less formal narrative of how increased income concentration at the top in the United States may have been a cause of the financial crisis of 2008 has been told by Raghuram Rajan in his *Fault Lines: How Hidden Fractures Still Threaten the World Economy*.[11]

---

9. See Carroll (2000); Cashell (2009); Dynan, Skinner, and Zeldes (2004). Others, however, have found different results. See, for example, Maki and Palumbo (2001).

10. Kumhof and Ranciere (2010; 2011).

11. Rajan (2010).

It is noteworthy that Rajan warned about the danger of financial crises as early as 2005 in a speech he delivered at a symposium in Jackson Hole, Wyoming, sponsored by the Federal Reserve Bank of Kansas City. Rajan argues that there are strong and understandable incentives in a democratic system to try to counteract the stagnation of middle and lower incomes and that these forces were at work in the United States before the financial crisis, when the government expanded its housing programs and the Federal Reserve slashed interest rates to forty-year lows in the first half of the 2000s. Both credit demand–side and credit supply–side factors worked in the same direction. On the credit supply side, the rich had more income than they could spend or invest directly in productive assets, so they were keen to invest in financial instruments promising a significant return. In a climate of abundant credit and low unemployment on the credit demand side, the middle- and lower-income groups were keen to compensate the stagnation of their real incomes by borrowing. The unsustainable increase of housing prices fueled by low interest rates and in part by various forms of government subsidy allowed and encouraged household borrowing because households believed their wealth had increased even though their income had not. The financial sector was happy to intermediate this process through the "originate and distribute" model, under which those originating the mortgages did not have to continue to carry them on their books and those holding them mistakenly believed that they were pooling unrelated risk. This led to a dangerous combination of excess supply of funds coming from the top layers of the income distribution (complemented by foreign funds attracted by the United States' safe haven status) and lack of income growth for the bottom 90 percent.[12]

Variations on this analysis and the story of all the government and regulatory failures that came with it have been told by several

12. Rajan (2010).

influential economists, including notably Joseph Stiglitz, Nouriel Roubini, Branko Milanovic, and Robert Reich.[13]

Despite the attention directed to the presumed link between income inequality and the making of the 2008 crisis, and the now wide-ranging debate on the political implications of income inequality, little attention has been paid to the question of how increased inequality may be affecting the present prospects for recovery and the effectiveness of macroeconomic policies. It could be argued that the United States is caught in a vicious cycle where a biting credit constraint at the middle and low end of the income distribution (dramatically exemplified by the large numbers of home foreclosures) has led to low expectations for effective demand growth and therefore low business investment. Monetary policy tries to stimulate demand with very low interest rates or "quantitative easing," or with both, but with dubious efficacy ("You can lead a horse to water, but you can't make it drink"), or at the risk of reigniting an unsustainable borrowing process by the bottom 90 percent. Moreover, very low interest rates may themselves worsen the distribution of income by leading to low or negative real returns for a large number of small savers, while companies can borrow at zero real rates and invest at much higher returns. Expansionary fiscal policy and increased spending on unemployment benefits and other elements of the social safety net are constrained by concerns about rising public debt. The United States may have reached a point where countercyclical policies have become much less effective in part because of a structural income concentration problem that limits sustainable growth in private demand. If this interpretation is correct, then rebalancing of the distribution of income may play a role in unlocking the U.S. economy's growth potential in a sustainable way.

13. See Nouriel Roubini, "Global Economic Insecurity and Inequality Breeds Social and Political Instability," 2011, Roubini Global Economics (www.roubini.com/analysis/164163.php; access by subscription); Reich (2010); Milanovic (2009); Stiglitz (2010); and, for a short summary, Dervis (2012).

Estimates of fiscal stimulus multipliers in the United States and elsewhere provide evidence in support of this view. Programs such as Food Stamps, unemployment benefits, and work-share, which provide transfers to boost the incomes of low-income or unemployed groups, are believed to be four to five times as effective in stimulating demand as policies that benefit high-income groups, such as tax cuts for those with high incomes, for corporations, and in capital gains.[14] Henry Ford recognized that it made sense to pay his workers enough so they could buy the cars they produced. An economy where nearly all of the income growth accrues to the very rich is unlikely to generate a corresponding growth in broad-based demand. Recent studies of the middle class in developing countries suggest that demand for nonessentials is greater and high growth is more likely to be sustained when the income distribution is more equal.[15] The link between increasing income inequality and the efficacy of traditional macroeconomic policies is a new area of research that requires more intensive examination.

Positional Goods and Cascading Expenditures

According to standard choice theory, people derive utility from their own consumption, and their self-interested pursuit of consumption can result in optimal outcomes for the community as a whole. The ideas underpinning behavioral economics, however, suggest this is not always the case. Robert Frank, in *The Darwin Economy,* provides copious examples of how relative consumption—one's own consumption relative to others'—plays a large role in determining the utility one derives from consumption.[16] Frank walks his reader through a thought experiment to demonstrate the point: "Would you rather live in a land where you had a 4,000-square-foot house and everyone else had a 6,000-square-foot

---

14. Zandi (2011).
15. Kharas (2010); Ali and Dadush (forthcoming).
16. Frank (2011).

house, or one in which you had a 3,000-square-foot house and everyone else had a 2,000-square-foot house? Given this choice, studies show that most respondents pick the latter. [Within certain limits] . . . they'd rather have less home in absolute terms if it means more home in relative terms." In other words, housing is a positional good—one where the neighbor's house matters and, as we discuss further, may lead everyone to want a bigger house than they otherwise would.

Does increased income inequality significantly affect the demand for positional goods? Frank and other economists in the behavioral school answer yes—relative consumption is actually important in many markets, not just housing. Economists have long been aware of the concept: the term was first coined by Fred Hirsch in 1976.[17] Luxury goods such as sports cars, boats, high-end clothing, and fine jewelry are obvious examples of positional goods. Less appreciated is the importance of positional services, such as where one sends one's children to school and the fact that the satisfaction one derives from a job may depend on how well paid it is compared to one's peers' pay. Frank argues that the prevalence of positional goods in society can cause large and preventable welfare loss through what he calls "positional externalities," a kind of "arms race" for positional goods as the bar for utility is continuously raised higher and higher. For clarity, one can take the extreme example of this cascading effect: a military arms race. In an armaments race, wasteful distortion is created when nations spend an enormous amount of resources building bombs, knowing that the adequacy of their arsenal can be assessed only in relation to the size to its rival's arsenal.

This bidding up of the value of positional goods, or the "expenditure cascade" down the income distribution, is exacerbated by greater income concentrations at the top. Frank argues that when top CEOs build larger and larger mansions, it "shifts the frame

17. Hirsch (1977).

of reference that defines acceptable housing for the near-rich, who travel in many of the same circles." This shift cascades downward to those families who are nearby in the income distribution, with the overall effect that everyone spends more on housing. There is some circumstantial evidence for Frank's contention: in 1980 the median new single-family house in the United States was 1,600 square feet; in 2007 it was more than 2,300 square feet. Yet we know that median family incomes have grown very little over the past thirty years. In essence, positional externalities expand both the demand and supply of many types of higher-end services and goods that are more expensive to produce

Positional goods interact with rising inequality in many ways. For example, the perceived increased need for these goods can affect norms about what a CEO "should" earn so as to keep up with her peers' lifestyle. Another locus where positional goods interact with income inequality to generate undesirable outcomes is the access to elite school education. It is well known which U.S. universities are considered to be the best and people are willing to pay substantial premiums for top-ranked university educations, so the price of attendance is pushed higher and higher. Those who attend are more likely to be children of wealthy parents, and are well placed to derive a big advantage in the marketplace from their "branded" education. Frank and Philip J. Cook use the more pedestrian example of the suit one wears to a job interview.[18] First impressions matter, and candidates with higher incomes can afford to pay substantially more than others for a good, even custom-tailored, suit; this then raises the reference frame for what is considered an appropriate interview suit. This expenditure sets off a cascade down the income distribution in which candidates feel that they must spend more money on their clothes if they are to compete for a job.

18. Frank and Cook (1995).

As explained by Frank, this concept of competition in consumption is based on Darwinian thought (relative consumption matters in a world where only the fittest survive) rather than on Adam Smith's ideas (only one's own consumption matters). It suggests that individual interests may diverge from what is best for the common good. Thus, just as when there are externalities in production—such as pollution—unfettered consumption competition is often inefficient and leads to the misallocation of resources, notably, in this case, the overproduction of positional goods. What is new about Frank's findings is that these externalities appear to be much more prevalent in society than classic economic theory suggests, affecting large swaths of consumption as well as production.

Societies have long experience in dealing with externalities in production, and have developed extensive regulations, taxes, and fines to discourage conditions such as pollution and unsafe workplaces. Externalities in consumption are a more recent discovery. It is interesting to note that a large group of countries that includes both European and developing countries make extensive use of luxury taxes—such as a higher-rate value-added tax that is applied to high-end automobiles—to disfavor positional goods. In the United States, by contrast, in at least one important area the tax system appears actually to favor positional goods: a mortgage interest tax deduction can now be taken for interest up to $1.1 million, about four times the price of the average American house.

4   THE CAUSES OF RISING INEQUALITY

IF THERE IS AGREEMENT on anything in the rich and varied literature on the causes of rising inequality and stagnant median incomes, it is that it is difficult to disentangle causes with any precision. A diverse set of factors—technology, trade, immigration, demographic shifts, and financialization, most of which are inextricably interwoven with policy and the political process—likely have contributed to the rise in inequality, but so far there is no consensus about the relative weight of each factor. For example, most economists would agree that increased international trade— made possible by improvements in communication and transportation technologies and by political decisions to open economies to trade—has not been by itself a major direct cause of stagnant wages or increased inequality in the United States (see later discussion under "Trade"). However, most economists would also agree that foreign competition, especially from low-wage countries, greatly increases the incentives to innovate and adopt laborsaving machinery, which does profoundly affect the job prospects of unskilled workers. Thus, technologies, trade-induced reallocation of resources, and political decisions to liberalize trade have a joint, and difficult to separate, effect on wages.

Still, even though the causes of inequality are difficult to identify with any precision, it is useful to consider each major factor in turn. Although many of the factors at work are not ones we could or even would want to reverse—for example, technological innovation—some might be. And in any event, policy can still aim to mitigate their effect on income inequality in other ways.

With this as background, in this chapter we briefly review some of what is known about the causes of inequality. For the purpose of exposition, we first discuss the economic drivers of inequality before turning, in chapter 5, to the complex relationship between politics and inequality. In practice, however, the economic causes of inequality discussed in this chapter and their relationships with policies and politics are a complex set of interacting factors and cannot be so cleanly categorized.

Technology

Skill-biased technological change (SBTC) is perhaps the most obvious suspect to identify as a cause for rising income inequality in the United States. As early as 1997 a Federal Reserve Bank of New York survey found that 45 percent of economists believed that technology had contributed to the increase in inequality over the previous two decades. Fewer than 15 percent of economists chose the next-most important factor, "Other."[1]

How does technology affect inequality? In 2002 the MIT economist Daron Acemoğlu noted that most economists believe that "technical change favors more skilled workers, replaces tasks previously performed by the unskilled, and exacerbates inequality."[2]

---

1. In addition to "other" and "technological change," the factors considered, in decreasing order of agreement, were "international trade," "decline in real minimum wage," "decline in unionization," and "rising immigration." Gilles Saint-Paul (2008) offers a rigorous, up-to-date theoretical analysis of the way technical progress affects inequality and wages. See also Council of Economic Advisers (1997).

2. Acemoğlu (2002).

Because increasingly sophisticated technology—comprising machine tools, computers, and robots—is able to replicate the routine cognitive and manual tasks performed by low-skilled labor but is (so far) unable to perform many of the more complex tasks required of high-skilled labor, computers reduce demand for members of the former group and increase it for members of the latter group.[3] Moreover, technology often complements the complex tasks performed by highly educated workers, increasing their productivity. This process, the argument goes, increases the wedge between workers of different skill levels and greatly increases the wage premium placed on education.

These trends are expected to continue to prevail in the future. For example, from 2008 to 2018, the U.S. Bureau of Labor Statistics expects the number of computer engineers in the United States to grow by 21 percent and the number of communications operators to fall by 10 percent, reflecting the introduction of "new labor-saving communications technologies."[4] At the same time, many low-pay jobs that provide a service rather than producing goods (such as janitors, waiters, security guards, and drivers) may be much less susceptible to automation, thus being protected to some degree.

There is much empirical and theoretical support for the belief that SBTC has played a significant role in hollowing out the labor force, increasing employment in jobs at the tails of the wage distribution at the expense of those in the middle. For example, David Autor, Frank Levy, and Richard Murnane have developed a model to describe computerization in labor markets. They find that technology was a significant if not leading cause for the increase in high-skilled labor demand from 1970 to 1998.[5]

---

3. Autor, Levy, and Murnane (2003).

4. U.S. Department of Labor, Bureau of Labor Statistics (2012).

5. Autor, Katz, and Kearney (2006); Autor (2010). Autor later argued that a similar phenomenon is occurring in other industrial countries.

Claudia Goldin and Lawrence Katz have also argued that this problem has been exacerbated by the decline in the supply of high-skilled labor, resulting from a slowdown in educational attainment over the last several decades, that has added to the increase in the wage premium for education.[6] They contrast the situation with pre-1970s twentieth-century trends, which saw educational attainment soar and inequality decline despite large-scale skill-based technological change in the form of electricity and automation. Recently, Erik Brynjolfsson and Andrew McAfee have taken up this theme in their book, *Race against the Machine: How the Digital Revolution Is Accelerating Innovation, Driving Productivity, and Irreversibly Transforming Employment in the Economy,* in which they postulate that inequality is increasing because the bulk of the population has not been able to improve its skills at a rate that matches technological change and reflects a different set of demands for labor.[7] Meanwhile, companies are still adjusting to the new information technologies, which means that in many instances the destruction of jobs has been proceeding more rapidly than the creation of new ones.

The effect of skill-based technological change is visible internationally, although in less pronounced fashion, perhaps because most countries, unlike the United States, have seen a surge in educational attainment over the last several decades. For example, the OECD concludes that technological change, when combined with globalization and political trends, has tended to increase income inequality in its member countries by increasing the demand for high-skilled labor relative to that for low-skilled labor.[8] From the mid-1980s to the late 2000s, the ratio of the 90th-percentile earner over the 10th-percentile earner increased by 0.46 percent a

---

6. Goldin and Katz (2009).
7. Brynjolfsson and McAfee (2011).
8. Organization for Economic Cooperation and Development (2011a, p. 110).

year; technological progress is estimated to account for about two thirds of that increase, according to OECD calculations.[9]

The substantial impact of technology on income dispersion could help explain the pronounced rise in inequality in United States, a country that is a leading force in science and technology. Despite being home to less than 5 percent of the world's population, the United States accounted for about a quarter of the world's patents in 2008 and scientific journal articles in 2007, while accounting for over 40 percent of its secure Internet servers in 2010. Similarly, from 2000 to 2009, U.S. high technology exports as a percentage of manufactures exports trailed those of only two OECD countries, Korea and Ireland.

Some economists, however, have doubts about the importance of technology in explaining the changes in the distribution of income. To start, despite the spread of similar technologies in other advanced countries, few if any other countries have seen inequality increase as sharply as the United States, suggesting that local factors are also at work. David Card and John DiNardo have pointed to a number of other flaws in the SBTC theory, noting, among other concerns, that technological progress continued to advance in the 1990s and 2000s, even though inequality growth during this period was concentrated at the very top of the distribution, rather than in the income ranges where one would expect SBTC to have the greatest impact.[10]

Trade

The belief is widespread that trade is a big culprit when it comes to job losses among low-skilled manufacturing workers, a view anchored in trade deficits and the inroads made by low-wage

---

9. Institutional and political changes accounted for a larger share of the increase (90 percent), whereas other factors—notably, rising education levels—reduced inequality.

10. Card and DiNardo (2002).

exporters in American markets. However, numerous careful attempts to quantify the effects of these trends on the relative demand for labor as well as the demand for skilled and unskilled workers have concluded that the effects are far too small to account for the big shifts in sectoral employment and relative wages that are observed in the United States. Instead, declines in the relative demand for goods and the increased demand for services as U.S. incomes rise, as well as skill-biased technological change that has enormously boosted the productivity of unskilled labor in manufacturing, provide quantitatively much more important explanations. As already discussed, there is, however, little doubt that the competition that comes with trade, including trade with low-wage imports, provides a big spur to labor-saving technological innovation, suggesting that the indirect effect of trade on inequality may be significant. For example, a recent analysis concluded that trade with China has greatly encouraged technical innovation in the United States and Europe.[11]

From the postwar period through the 1970s, U.S. trade (imports and exports) was for the most part in balance. In the mid-1980s, a sizable current account deficit, driven largely by the trade deficit, emerged, and it was on an upward trend until the Great Recession hit.[12] The large trade deficit in the United States over most of the past thirty years makes it plausible that more jobs were lost in industries competing with imports than were gained in export industries, although it is not possible to state this categorically without taking into account the relative labor intensities of these industries. However, various studies have concluded that the association between trade deficits and employment and

11. See Bloom, Draca, and Van Reenen (2011). For a more detailed discussion of the links between trade and technology, see Grossman and Helpman (1995).

12. The current account balance is largely a function of the trade balance but it also reflects net factor income from abroad (earnings on foreign investment minus payments made to foreign investors) and cash transfers. A negative current account balance must be financed by foreign savings.

FIGURE 4-1. U.S. International Trade in Goods and Services

Billions of U.S.$

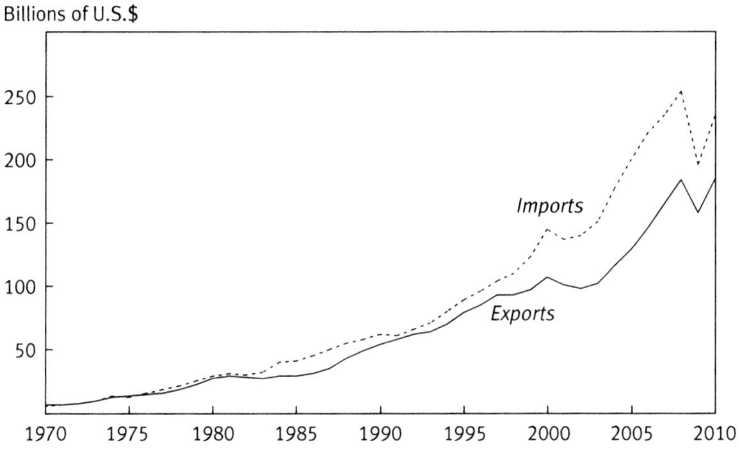

Source: U.S. Census Bureau, U.S. International Trade in Goods and Services (FT900It was taken from the FT900 tables, so no date (www.census.gov/foreign-trade/Press-Release/current_press_release/).

relative labor demand is small.[13] Moreover, current account deficits are the endogenous result of aggregate savings and investment decisions, which are affected by many variables of which foreign competition is just one. For example, the biggest surge in the current account deficit occurred in the period from 2000 to 2006, from 4.2 percent to 6 percent of GDP, but this period was also characterized by low unemployment in the United States—the average unemployment rate over the period was 5 percent and never went above 6.3 percent (see figure 4-1). This suggests that the widening current account deficit was the result of a domestic spending boom rather than increased foreign competition per se.

The portion of U.S. imports of manufactured goods from developing countries with an abundance of low-wage workers has risen

13. See, for example, Lawrence and Bailey (2004) and Krugman (1995). For a discussion on the data surrounding these issues, see U.S. Government Accountability Office (2004).

FIGURE 4-2. U.S. International Trade in Goods and Services

Percent of GDP

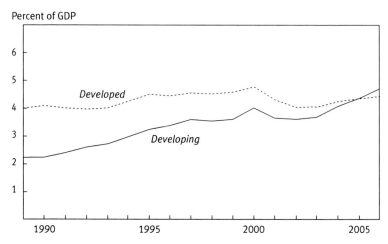

Source: Krugman (2008, p. 105).

substantially since the end of the 1980s (see figure 4-2). In 1979, imports from low-wage countries represented only 1.6 percent of GDP; by 1989, this percentage had increased only slightly, to 2 percent. In 2000, however, low-wage imports increased significantly, to 5.1 percent of GDP. By 2010 they accounted for more than half all manufactured imports.[14] Between 1979 and 2010, the total increase in the trade deficit in manufactures was 5.4 percent of U.S. GDP. This accounts for a little less than half of the decline in manufactures' share of GDP over the period, illustrating the importance of demand factors in accounting for the slow growth of manufactures. The employment share in manufactures declined by more than the value-added share, reflecting increased productivity and illustrating the importance of technology.

14. United Nations Commodity Trade Statistics Database (http://comtrade. un.org).

It is also important to stress that although the predominant focus in the political debate is on shrinking employment opportunities, manufactured imports from developing countries also imply lower prices for all U.S. consumers, including unskilled workers, who are more likely to buy the basic manufactures exported by these countries.[15]

More recently attention has focused on the fact that growth in U.S. imports from China, now the world's largest exporter, are not only in unskilled-labor-intensive industries such as apparel and accessories; a substantial amount of the increase is also attributed to computer and electronic products, which are skilled-labor intensive (see figure 4-3). But some of the know-how and skill embodied in these "Chinese" products actually reflect imports from the United States and other advanced countries in the complex value chain that leads to the final product. There are competing viewpoints on how all this has impacted U.S. workers.

Jared Bernstein, Lawrence Mishel, and Heidi Shierholz suggest that the rising imports in the skilled-labor-intensive computer and electronics industry may indicate that this kind of work is being moved offshore. If this is the case, then not only are low-skilled workers at risk, but also the so-called "winners" in globalization, highly educated workers, may be at risk.[16] Paul Krugman, however, points out that the rise in the imports of computer and electronic products is actually in large part a statistical illusion— the export data do not represent value added since a large part of exports consist of imported components that are assembled into subsequent-stage products. In other words, the rise in the imports of skilled-labor-intensive goods such as electronics and computers from China and other developing and emerging countries may be overstated because many of the more advanced components to the final product were imported from other countries, including

15. Broda and Romalis (2008).
16. Bernstein, Mishel, and Shierholz (2009, p. 193).

FIGURE 4-3. Value Added by Industry as a Percent of GDP

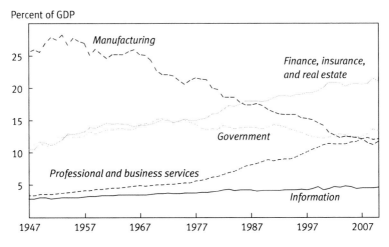

Percent of GDP

Source: U.S. Bureau of Economic Analysis (release date April 26, 2011).

the United States and other developed countries. In 2002 Judith
Dean, K. C. Fung, and Zhi Wang estimated that 57 percent of the
value of Chinese computers exported abroad came from imported
inputs.[17] For example, if components made mostly in Japan are
used in China to assemble a computer that is then exported to the
United States, the import is classified as coming from China while
in reality a large portion of the price of the good reflects skilled-
labor-intensive inputs from Japan—whose factor prices, such as
labor, land, and capital, are similar to those of the United States.[18]

All other advanced countries have seen large increases in trade
with developing countries in recent years; in fact, the trade share
of U.S. GDP is only about one third that of other OECD countries.
The level of trade integration, defined as the sum of imports and
exports as a share of GDP, in OECD countries has doubled over

17. Dean, Fung, and Wang (2007).
18. Krugman (2008).

the past thirty years. An OECD report published in 2011 finds that less than one quarter of the total increase in merchandise imports into OECD countries came from developing countries. The report finds that, despite the greater prevalence of trade in the average OECD country than in the United States, trade integration has not had a statistically significant impact on wage inequality, though the report notes that countries with weak employment protection, such as the United States, experience heightened wage dispersion due to these shifts in trade (see figure 4-4).[19]

Immigration

The United States is a nation of immigrants, yet worries about immigration are widespread, and in the popular imagination immigration plays a large role in depressing wages and taking jobs away from the U.S.-born. Yet a large number of studies have indicated only a weak link between immigration and the wages of U.S.-born workers.

The proportion of the foreign–born population in the United States has grown substantially since 1970 (see figure 4-5).[20] It is estimated that the growth in the number of foreign-born workers relative to the U.S.-born labor force has increased drastically over the past four decades. In 1970 the foreign-born population made up approximately 5.2 percent of the civilian labor force.[21] This share increased to 6.5 percent in 1980 and to 8.8 percent by 1990. In 2000 the foreign-born population made up 12.4 percent

19. Organization for Economic Cooperation and Development (2011b).

20. The Census Bureau defines "foreign-born" as people residing in the United States on census day who were not born in the United States. The foreign-born have a variety of immigration statuses and include immigrants, temporary migrants, refugees, non-immigrants, and persons illegally residing in the United States.

21. The United States Bureau of Labor Statistics defines the civilian labor force as all individuals age sixteen or older who are neither in an institution (such as a correctional facility, mental health care facility, or nursing home) nor on active duty in the armed forces.

FIGURE 4-4. Change in Trade Intensity, by Region of Origin, 1980–2008[a]

Panel A. Import intensity (imports/GDP)

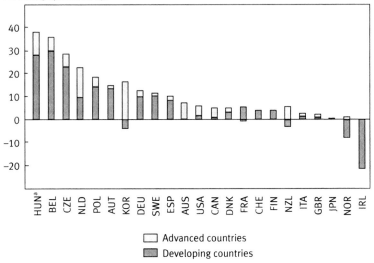

Panel B. Export intensity (exports/GDP)

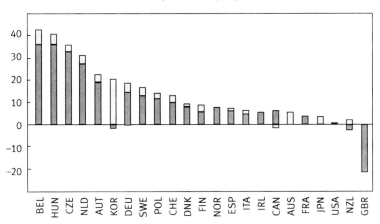

Source: Organization for Economic Cooperation and Development (2011b, p. 89).
a. Data series begins in early 1990s. Trade in services is not included.

FIGURE 4-5. U.S.- and Foreign-Born Population Sizes, 1850–2008

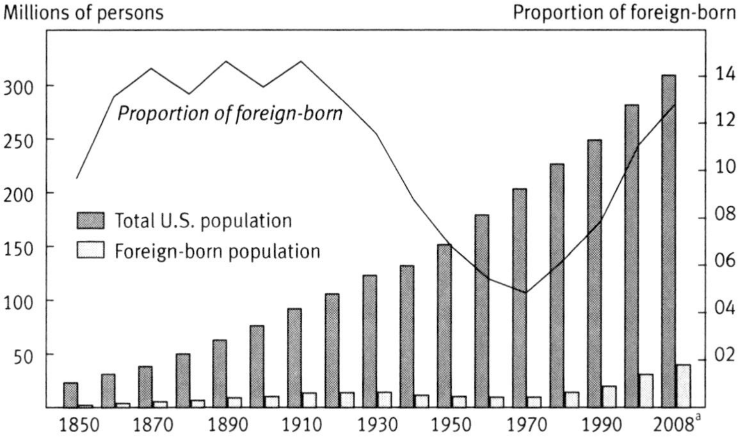

Millions of persons   Proportion of foreign-born

Source: Kandel (2011, p. 2).
a. The foreign-born proportion of 12.5 percent for 2008 is not shown because the decade is incomplete.

of the civilian labor force and in 2008 this number increased substantially, to 15.7 percent, with Mexican immigration accounting for 44 percent of the growth of immigrant labor.[22] Note that these rates do not consider labor-force participation rates for the foreign-born and U.S.-born workforce. Data show that these rates differ significantly within different subgroups of the population, such as by gender and age.

A rise in the number of foreign-born workers increases the availability of labor in the United States. As of 2010, 26.5 percent of the foreign-born labor force over the age of twenty-five had less than a high school education, so U.S.-born workers who share similar education profiles are the ones most likely to be affected by rising immigration. As of 2010, only 5.4 percent of the native-born labor force over the age of twenty-five did not hold a high school

22. Kandel (2011); Bernstein, Mishel, and Shierholz (2009, p. 197).

diploma. Of course, when the number of foreign-born workers increases, it also has some effect on the supply of workers with higher levels of education, so the mix of these workers would be important in determining the effect on the income distribution.[23]

Although some economists have found a significant link between immigration and wages, most empirical studies have found this link to be weak. For example, George J. Borjas concludes that immigration has had a significant negative impact on competing workers' wages. By contrast, Gianmarco I. P. Ottaviano and Giovanni Peri find that immigration has had a significant *positive* effect on wages for skilled U.S. workers and a small negative effect on wages for unskilled workers, while David Card finds little connection between immigration and wages for less-educated native workers.[24] There are a number of possible explanations for the weakness of the link between migration and U.S. wages. First, foreign-born workers and U.S.-born workers may not be interchangeable, especially at the low end of skills. Foreign-born unskilled workers often speak inadequate English and are willing to do jobs U.S.-born workers will not do. Foreign-born workers can complement U.S.-born workers by giving companies the opportunity to use capital investment and land most effectively. For example, farmers in California depend crucially on foreign-born workers for the most arduous tasks. The foreign-born population also adds to aggregate demand, including the demand for housing; they also contribute to the welfare of all Americans by reducing the price of personal services, construction, and infrastructure.

In short, the currently available data do not allow us to determine the impact of immigration on absolute wages and employment with any precision, as the conclusions of numerous studies differ. The impact—positive or negative—of moderate immigration on U.S.-born workers with similar education profiles is unlikely to be large.

---

23. Bernstein, Mishel, and Shierholz (2009).
24. See Borjas (2003); Ottaviano and Peri (2006); Card (2005).

Demographic Changes

Over the past several decades, the U.S. labor force has seen two seismic demographic shifts. First, marriage rates have fallen dramatically. From 1960 to 2011, the proportion of employed men who are married and living with their spouses fell steadily from 79 percent to 58 percent, with the sharpest declines at the lowest income levels. Because incomes of single-parent households are among the most unequally distributed, the falling marriage rate has likely contributed to the increase in inequality of household income.[25]

The second major shift in the U.S. workforce was the increased participation of women. From 1960 through 1990, female employment rose considerably faster than male employment as women entered the workforce. Over that period, women accounted for 60 percent of civilian-labor-force growth; their share of the workforce rose from 33 percent to 45 percent. Since 1990, the growth in women's share of the labor force has slowed: in 2011 they accounted for 47 percent of workers, close to half, suggesting the end of this trend.

Increased female employment has been accompanied by women's increased educational achievement and rising pay. From 1979 to 2009, wages of women rose from 62 percent to 80 percent of men's wages. The percentage for younger cohorts—those from sixteen to twenty-four and then, as this groups ages, between twenty-five and thirty-five—rose to 90 percent and then leveled off. This suggests that the wage gap will continue to narrow as wages equalize for older cohorts—that is, as younger cohorts age. In addition, in 1970, 40 percent of college graduates were women (lower, in fact, than in 1940) and 48 percent of those starting college were female. By 2010, 51 percent of the country's college graduates and 56 percent of college freshmen were females.

25. Western, Bloome, and Percheski (2008); Daly and Valletta (2004).

It is unclear how these shifts have affected inequality. Several studies have found that increasing participation and wages among females have partially offset the rise in male wage inequality, reducing household income inequality in the United States by as much as 25 percent.[26]

Others have reached different conclusions. Because of the sharp fall in marriage rates among low-income men, members of this group are actually less likely to be married to a working spouse, despite the increase in female workforce participation. Though the marriage rate also declined among high-income men, their marriage rate to working women rose. Thus, by increasing the correlation between spouses' incomes, rising female workforce participation may actually have added to income inequality.[27]

Analyses across different countries reveals that inequality-reducing factors tend to outweigh inequality-increasing factors in many countries, but not in the United States. The OECD found that, in twenty-three member countries, increasing female employment lowered the Gini coefficient by an average of 1.2 percentage points from the mid-1980s to the mid-2000s. Changes in household structures (more single households) and "assortative mating" (people marrying spouses with similar incomes) increased the Gini by an average of 0.3 and 0.7 percentage points, respectively; thus, these changes where, on net, an equalizing force in the group. With regard to the United States the OECD comes to the opposite conclusion. Though the increase in single households and "assortative mating" rates in the United States are on par with OECD averages, female employment rose by less than half of the OECD average (partly reflecting relatively high female employment rates in the mid-1980s). Consequently, increasing female employment had a less dramatic equalizing effect on income inequality in the

---

26. Daly and Valletta (2004); Pencavel (2006); Cancian and Reed (1998); Western, Bloome, and Percheski (2008).

27. Burtless (1999).

United States—the OECD estimates it lowered the Gini coefficient by 0.4 percentage points—and the net effect of the three changes was mildly positive, an increase of 0.3 percentage points.

Winner-Take-All Markets

Winner-take-all markets are defined as "markets in which small differences in performance (or even small differences in the credentials used to predict performance) translate into extremely large differences in reward."[28] Classic winner-take-all markets include sports and entertainment, where there can be only one winner of a golf tournament and one actor in the starring role—think Tiger Woods and George Clooney. Even the person in second place may get nothing, or a fraction of the winner's earnings.

Globalization, television, and the collapse in communications costs have meant that the rewards in many winner-take-all markets have surged, as they can now reach a global audience, whereas they once could only reach a few hundred at one time. Meanwhile the phenomenon has become much more prevalent. Consider a commodities broker hiring a senior trader for its operations. The volume of financial transactions has exploded with electronic trading, globalization, and financialization. Trading firms often rely on speed tests to try to measure how quickly and accurately the job candidate responds to available opportunities. Suppose this firm were deciding between two candidates, one who answered sixty-five questions correctly in eight minutes and the other who answered sixty questions correctly in eight minutes. The successful candidate will be responsible for a portfolio of investments of more than $400 million. If she can make slightly better decisions and conceivably contribute, say, around 1 percent more than the other candidate to the company's profit—about $4 million dollars—the company can easily justify paying

---

28. Cook and Frank (1995, p. 144). See also Saint-Paul (2008).

the slightly faster trader a one-million-dollar salary, whereas the slower candidate may end up in a job earning a fraction of that. Technological innovation has expanded the scope of winner-take-all markets. Take, for example, the Wimbledon tennis tournament, a typical example of a winner-take-all market in which the winner takes home twice as much as the other finalist and four times as much as the semifinalist—and can, in addition, look forward to very large financial rewards from sponsorship deals. In 1970, long before live TV coverage and Web streaming to personal computers, the winner of the Wimbledon tournament played in front of a modest audience and received £47,733. In 2010, with viewers tuned in from around the world, the men's champion received £919,701, and the income from global sponsorship deals could be many times that.[29] Of course, elite tennis players are few in number and thus unlikely to contribute greatly to income inequality measured across the whole income distribution. Nevertheless, the increase in the number of winner-take-all markets is important to rising income inequality, from the CEOs of medium-sized and large companies to software developers to Silicon Valley entrepreneurs to traders.

Winner-take-all markets also spur feedback mechanisms that can promote even greater inequality. The top-paid employees in one market generally demand other top-paid employees' products. For example, the successful financial trader calls for the best dentist, purchases the best luxury car, and hires the best cosmetic surgeon. As a result the prices for good dental services, luxury cars, and cosmetic surgery have increased, providing the relatively best providers of such services and goods with greater incomes, making inequality even more entrenched.

---

29. Earnings calculated in terms of 2005 British pounds sterling, accounting for inflation (see www.wimbledon.com/heritage/history/prize-money).

Financialization

"Financialization" is a relatively new term that refers to the growth of the centrality of the finance sector in the operation of the economy and governing institutions. The economist Thomas Palley suggests the core impacts of financialization are to "(1) elevate the significance of the financial sector relative to the real sector, (2) transfer income from the real sector to the financial sector, and (3) increase income inequality and contribute to wage stagnation."[30] The conduits of financialization, it has been proposed, include changes in the structure and operation of financial markets, changes in corporate behavior that have facilitated the decline in union power and encouraged a culture of debt finance, and changes in economic policies so as to promote financial sector interests.[31]

Data from the United States support these hypotheses to at least some degree. Since 1979 the size of the financial sector as a percentage of GDP has increased drastically, coinciding with the dramatic decline in the manufacturing sector. In 1957 manufacturing accounted for 27 percent of total U.S. GDP, whereas finance, insurance, and real estate (FIRE) accounted for approximately 13 percent. By 2008 these proportions had almost completely reversed: manufacturing accounted for 12 percent of GDP while FIRE's share stood at 20 percent (see figure 4-6). Financial sector debt has grown much more rapidly than either corporate or household debt, providing further evidence of the financialization of the U.S. economy (see figure 4-7).

The historical sociologist Greta R. Krippner has defined financialization as a pattern in which profits are generated mostly through financial interactions rather than through trade and

---

30. Palley (2007, p. 3).
31. See, for example, Palley (2007); Whalen and Zalewski (2010); Bernstein, Mishel, and Shierholz (2009); Cowen (2011).

FIGURE 4-6. Total Credit Market Debt Owned, by Sector, 1960–2009

Percent of GDP

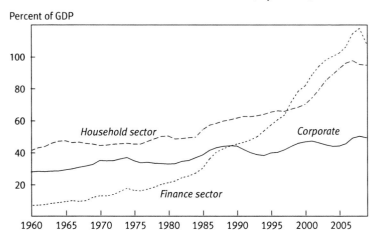

Source: Authors' calculations, based on Council of Economic Advisers (1997, table B-1) and Maki and Pallumbo (2001, table L.1).

production. We have indeed seen a sharp amplification of this process since about 1950.[32] Krippner has quantified this empirical fact by measuring the differences between portfolio income and corporate cash flow and expressing them as a ratio. She defines portfolio income as earnings from interest, dividends, and realized capital gains, and corporate cash flows as profits plus depreciation allowances. The higher the ratio of portfolio income to cash flow, the more advanced is the process of financialization of non-financial companies. Using Krippner's definitions we can see the increase in the ratio of portfolio income to cash flow for U.S. nonfinancial companies between 1950 and 2001, shown in figure 4-7.

Beginning in the 1980s the United States undertook a strategy of massively deregulating capital markets, referred to by Richard Freeman and others as a "giant laissez-faire experiment."[33]

32. Krippner (2005, p. 174).
33. See, for example, Richard Freeman (2010).

FIGURE 4-7. Ratio of Portfolio Income to Cash Flow,
U.S. Nonfinancial Firms

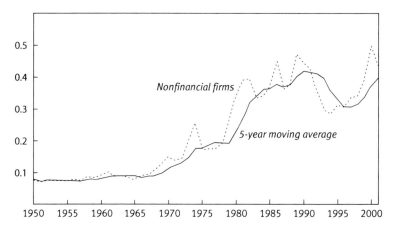

Source: Krippner (2005, p. 185) (used by permission of Oxford University Press).

Facing little oversight and weak regulations, finance firms created increasingly complicated and opaque financial instruments
to maximize profits. Corporations became more dependent on
capital markets and less on traditional bank lending. Setting aside
for the moment the effects of the deregulation of capital markets
on the rest of the economy, it resulted in a rapid rise in growth,
profits, and earnings for finance firms and the financiers who
managed them. This shift changed management incentives in various ways.[34] With the rapid rise of financial markets and the associated rise in arm's-length arrangements—arrangements between
unrelated parties that are enforced through contracts and based
on publicly available information—shareholders moved toward
placing increased value on short-term profitability. Coupled with
this short-term focus was a change in the compensation structure
for executives to one in which most of their compensation was in

34. See Crotty (2009).

the form of stock options and bonuses that reward excessive risk taking. In order for management to make money on their options or get their bonuses, they needed to report company finances that continuously increased the company's share price. In essence, incentives for rent-seeking behavior dominated, providing a big upside for financiers and no downside. The moral hazard associated with the "too big to fail" syndrome in banks and other financial institutions also contributed to excessive risk taking in the financial sector.

The idea that financialization is "bad" may seem counterintuitive—after all, financial markets play a crucial role in resource allocation in market economies. The problem is the tendency of financial markets—reflecting information asymmetries and crowd behavior—to move in boom-bust cycles, which is one of the most persistent empirical features and is also one that has been extensively studied.[35] These extreme swings can cause tremendously costly economic crises. Moreover, the rise of financialization appears to have weakened the focus on long-term capital allocation and strengthened it on short-term bets and speculation that employs high leverage. Credit market debt held by the household, corporate nonfinancial, and financial sectors reached its highest point on record in early 2009 (total credit market debt, which includes public debt, also reached a peak in the first quarter of 2009, at around 390 percent of GDP). This trend was particularly sharp for the financial sector, where credit market debt nearly tripled, from 43 percent of GDP in 1990 to nearly 110 percent of GDP in 2009 (see figure 4-6).[36]

In addition to being potentially destabilizing, financialization has been associated directly with increased income inequality. To start with, the financial sector is overrepresented among the country's top earners: in 1979, the financial sector accounted for

35. See, for example, Minsky (1993).
36. Crotty (2005).

5.4 percent of U.S. employees, and accounted for 7.7 percent of earners in the top 1 percent (excluding capital gains earnings). By 2005 the financial sector accounted for 6.1 percent of all workers but for 13.9 percent of the top 1 percent of earners. Among the top 0.1 percent of the income distribution, the financial sector's share was even higher, rising from 11 to 18 percent between 1979 and 2005.[37] A 2011 report by the Institute for Policy Studies reports that the ratio between CEO and worker pay has risen from 42:1 in 1980, to 107:1 in 1990, to 325:1 in 2010.[38] The growth of the financial sector has also facilitated the shift in income composition away from wages toward capital gains, which are more unequal, contributing further to the concentration of income at the top of the distribution. Many authors such as Tyler Cowen argue that financialization has also created a winner-take-all phenomenon that provides huge rewards to small groups of investors.[39]

The enormous pay differentials between jobs in the finance sector and other sectors of the economy have also attracted increasingly larger shares of new graduates from top universities to compete for a limited number of jobs. This shift of human capital away from other sectors of the "real" economy to the finance sector is one of the most flagrant examples of winner-take-all markets as described by Frank.[40] Managers and CEOs who arguably are only marginally better than their peers often enjoy enormous salary advantages.

37. Bakija, Cole, and Heim (2010).

38. See Anderson and others (2011). Note that the total executive compensation figures include salary, bonuses, perks, above-market interest on deferred compensation, and the value of stock and option awards. Worker pay is based on U.S. Department of Labor, Bureau of Labor Statistics Current Employment Statistics Survey, which measures the average hourly earnings of production workers (www.bls.gov/ces/).

39. Cowen (2011).

40. Frank (2011).

5 POLICY, POLITICS, AND INEQUALITY

NO TREATMENT OF THE causes of inequality in the United States is complete without discussion of the role politics played in shaping the trends that affect inequality and of the role that large concentrations of income at the top play in influencing policies. The latter phenomenon is especially important in the United States because of the high cost of political campaigns and the prevalence of lobbies in shaping legislation. As Senator Mark Hanna famously quipped in the 1890s, "There are two things that are important in politics. The first is money, and I can't remember what the second one is."[1]

How Politics Affects Inequality

The U.S. government has the ability to influence income distribution through numerous channels. Most important, the government—particularly the federal government—can directly alter the income distribution in the United States through its power to tax and spend. As is typical in all advanced countries, the United States uses some of this power to reduce income inequality by

1. Sam Roberts, "Lesson in Politics: Role of Credibility," *New York Times*, Metro Matters, September 20, 1993.

FIGURE 5-1. Percent Reduction in Income Inequality
(as Shown by the Gini Index) from Transfers and Federal Taxes

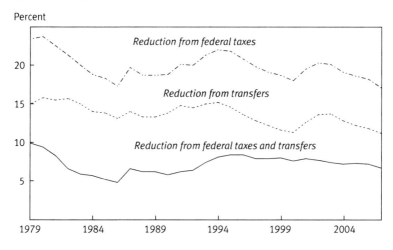

Source: Congressional Budget Office (2011).

taxing higher earners at higher rates and providing direct financial support to poor and disadvantaged groups via transfers.
These taxes and transfers are significant: the Congressional Budget Office (CBO) estimated in a 2011 report that these policies
lowered the Gini index by about 20 percent in 2007. However,
the government's redistributive role, through both transfers and
taxes, has been diminishing over time: as the CBO noted, both
shifts in government transfers and federal taxes have contributed
to the rise of post-tax and transfers income inequality in recent
years (see figure 5-1).[2]

Over the decades since 1980 the focus of transfer programs
has shifted away from the poor and toward the elderly, who
tend to be wealthier than the average of the population. As programs such as Social Security and Medicare, which are not means-
tested, have expanded, lower-income households have received

2. CBO (2011).

FIGURE 5-2. Top Marginal U.S. Tax Rate

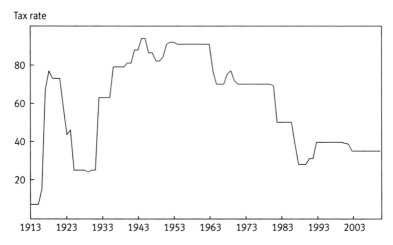

Source: Tax Policy Center, "Historical Top Tax Rate," April 13, 2012 (www.taxpolicycenter.org/tax facts/displayafact.cfm?Docid=213).

less government assistance, despite a small overall rise in total transfer payments. As a result, the percentage of total transfers received by households in the bottom income quintile fell from 54 percent in 1979 to 36 percent in 2007.

Taxes have also become less progressive and are sometimes actually regressive. Since the 1960s the top marginal tax rate has declined dramatically. Marginal tax rates do not represent actual tax burdens, so this rate taken alone can be misleading. Real effective tax rates, the tax rate one pays assuming that one pays a flat rate rather than under a progressive system, have fallen for all income levels: from 1979 to 2005, the tax rate for the top 0.1 percent of earners fell from 42.9 to 31.5 percent, while rates on the lowest quintile fell from 8.0 to 4.3 percent. Thus, the change in effective tax rates has also had a regressive impact on income after taxes.

The CBO finds that shifts in the *composition* of federal taxes are also making their overall effect less progressive. Since 1979, federal taxes shifted away from income taxes, which are progressive, toward payroll taxes (social insurance taxes as a percentage of household income, including transfers), which are regressive. The net effect has been regressive, according to the CBO.

An analysis by the Organization for Economic Cooperation and Development confirms the CBO's analysis. The OECD study, which looks at just working-age populations in twelve advanced countries, finds that taxes and transfers have become more redistributive in its member countries, but not in the United States.[3] In these countries, taxes and transfers lowered market income inequality (as measured by the Gini) by an average of 26 percent in the mid-1980s and by 29 percent in the mid-2000s. Corroborating the CBO analysis, the OECD found that in the United States the redistributive effect fell from 20 percent in 1979 to 18 percent in 2004.[4]

Our interpretation of the data reported by the OECD study leads to the conclusion that redistributive policies in the United States are weak largely because of low spending on benefits, which have a much stronger impact on inequality than do taxes. In the mid-2000s, U.S. households headed by a working-age individual paid 25 percent of their market income in direct taxes, slightly less than the OECD average, but received only 5 percent of their income in benefits, one third of the OECD average. The effects of this are particularly noticeable at the lower end of the income distribution, which tends to be less affected by tax policy than higher sections of the income distribution but much more affected by government transfers, such as unemployment benefits and Medicaid.

An important additional point is that focusing on actual tax receipts and expenditures gives only a very partial picture of the

3. See Organization for Economic Cooperation and Development (2011b). The OECD, by restricting its analysis to people age fifteen to sixty-four, focused on interpersonal redistribution and not intergenerational transfers.

4. Australia, Canada, Denmark, Finland, West Germany, Israel, Netherlands, Norway, Sweden, Switzerland, United Kingdom, and United States.

FIGURE 5-3. Nominal Wage and Real Minimum Wage in 2011 Prices

Nominal and real minimum wage

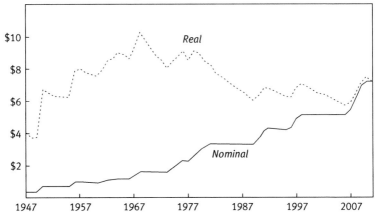

Source: Authors' calculations based on U.S. Department of Labor, "History of Federal Minimum Wage Rates under the Fair Labor Standards Act, 1938–2009" (www.dol.gov/whd/minwage/chart. htm), and the Bureau of Labor Statistics Consumer Price Index (www.bls.gov/cpi/cpirsdc.htm).

redistributive effects of government policies. The so-called "tax expenditures," namely, tax exemptions, or offsets such as the mortgage interest deduction or the "carried interest" provision of the U.S. tax code that treats many forms of private equity and hedge fund incomes as long-term capital gains—taxed at a lower rate than regular income—constitute regressive components of overall government tax policies, with significant consequences for the distribution of disposable incomes.

Changes in government regulations also play a role in distribution of income. For example, cross-state analysis shows that the decline in the federal minimum wage—which in real terms fell to its lowest level in over fifty years in 2006—may have had a substantial impact on the rise in income inequality, essentially by depressing income at the low-end of the distribution (see figure 5-3).[5]

5. Lee (1999).

Some have argued that de-unionization has contributed to the rise in inequality. Casual observation suggests that there is some truth in this. According to the Bureau of Labor Statistics (BLS), the U.S. union membership rate (defined as the percentage of wage and salary workers who are members of a union) declined from 20.1 percent in 1983 to 11.8 percent in 2011. Unionization can have a substantial impact on income: among twenty-one occupational groups reported on by the BLS, eighteen groups' members receive a higher weekly income if they are in a union—by an average of over 25 percent. Moreover, the three groups whose unionized members receive a lower salary than their non-unionized counterparts are the three highest-paid groups. More systematic statistical analysis provides further support for this view. For example, de-unionization explains a significant part of the rise of male wage inequality, according to the economists David Card, Thomas Lemieux, and W. Craig Riddell (they conclude that de-unionization has had little effect on female inequality).[6]

Research carried out at the OECD corroborates the view that policy changes contribute to the rise in U.S. inequality. Across the OECD, unionization has decreased while employment protection legislation and product market regulation has weakened—trends found to be associated with increased inequality. Other factors, such as lower unemployment insurance replacement rates and lower minimum wages, are also correlated with higher inequality. In the aggregate, the OECD finds that these political and institutional changes have been the most powerful driving force behind the rise in inequality. From the mid-1980s to the mid-2000s, they increased the ratio of incomes of the top 10 percent of households over that of the bottom 10 percent by 0.42 percent annually, compared to an observed increase of 0.47 percent annually. (Technological progress, the second most important factor, added another 0.32 percent to the ratio annually. Meanwhile, increasing

6. Card, Lemieux, and Riddell (2003).

education levels had a significant offsetting effect: lowering the ratio by about 0.5 percent annually.)

How Inequality Affects Politics

Government policies play a major role in shaping inequality. There is considerable evidence that increased income concentration at the top has been associated with the adoption of policies that favor the wealthy. Jacob S. Hacker and Paul Pierson provide a series of arguments and examples showing how the policy design and implementation process is often shaped by the interests of the very highest-income groups.[7] Their argument is that the age of "winner-take-all markets" is also an age of "winner-take-all politics." Moreover, there is also evidence of a link between income inequality and polarization in politics. For example, a *Washington Post* article reported on work showing that the rise in income inequality has closely tracked the rise in congressional polarization as measured by voting along party lines.[8] A further factor contributing to inequality, according to the political scientists Alfred Stepan and Juan Linz, is that checks and balances and various forms of veto powers in the United States, which are stronger than in any other long-standing democracy, limit the ability of the majority to pursue their agenda, a circumstance that would tend to result in policies that reduce income inequality.[9] This suggests that technical, institutional reforms such as abolishing the Senate filibuster could be a significant step toward reducing inequality.

According to Frank Levy and Peter Temin, there has been a shift in political norms away from what they call the Treaty

7. Hacker and Pierson (2010).

8. Peter Whoriskey, "Growing Wealth Widens Distance between Lawmakers and Constituents," *Washington Post*, December 26, 2011.

9. Stepan and Linz (2011).

of Detroit—the "general government effort to broadly distribute the gains from growth"—toward policies of deregulation and privatization that encourage efficiency without much regard for distribution.[10] Similarly, Paul Krugman argues in *Conscience of a Liberal* that shifting political attitudes were central to the rise in inequality.[11] Jeffrey Sachs, in his recent book, *The Price of Civilization: Reawakening American Virtue and Prosperity*, also contends that powerful interests strongly influence the U.S. political system and that this has allowed inequality to rise to current levels.[12]

The thesis advanced by these various authors—that aggregate political influence can buy wealth, and has been doing so for a long time—leads to the troubling implication that income concentration at the top can become self-reinforcing through capture of the political system. High income leads to more political influence, which in turn leads to higher income. Although it takes more than money to win political office in the United States, money clearly helps. Most office seekers in the United States fund their campaigns through private contributions rather than public sources of election funding, because they can raise much more funds from private donors if they forgo public funds restricted by a ceiling. These private contributions, the restraints on which are being eroded in various ways, often come from the very wealthy.[13] In the 2010 case *Citizens United* v. *Federal Election Commission*, the U.S. Supreme Court struck down laws that limited political spending by corporations. With candidates now raising record amounts of money—the expectation is that the 2012 presidential

10. Levy and Temin (2007).
11. Krugman (2007).
12. Sachs (2011).
13. Dan Eggen and T. W. Farnam, "New 'Super Pacs' Bringing Millions into Campaigns," *Washington Post*, September 28, 2010; Miller (2011).

campaign will cost more than $2 billion—it is not difficult to see how wealthy contributors may gain disproportionate influence.[14] Money can provide disproportionate influence in other ways. In 2010, individuals, corporations, unions, and other groups spent $3.5 billion lobbying the federal government—up from $1.4 billion in 1998. Lobbies serve a wide range of interests, including environmental causes and civil rights, but the top-spending lobbies in 2010 were pharmaceuticals, electric utilities, business associations, insurance, and the oil and gas industries. In 2010 the top spender was the U.S. Chamber of Commerce, which spent nearly three times what the second largest spender, the Pacific Gas and Electric Company, a California electric utility, spent.[15]

Campaign finance, lobbying, and even the composition of the U.S political class, in combination, appear to have strongly tilted outcomes toward the interests of the very wealthy. It may be true, as the political scientist Martin Gilens wrote in 2005, that for much of the three decades since 1980, U.S. policy decisions have largely reflected a "consensus" across the public at large. But Gilens also found that when opinion differs by income group, "actual policy outcomes strongly reflect the preferences of the most affluent but bear virtually no relationship to the preferences of poor or middle-income Americans."[16] Others have reached similar conclusions.[17]

Many have pointed to the growth of the financial sector as an example of the mutually reinforcing relationship between the

14. See, for example, the National Institute on Money in State Politics, "myFollowTheMoney" (database available at www.followthemoney.org/data base/IndustryTotals.phtml) and Peter Overby, "2012: The Year of the Billion-Dollar Campaigns?" National Public Ratio, February 18, 2011 (www.npr.org/2011/02/18/133809150/2012-the-year-of-the-billion-dollar-campaigns).

15. See Center for Responsive Politics, "Super PACs Cast Long Shadow over 2012 Race," March 21, 2011 (www.opensecrets.org).

16. Gilens (2005).

17. Bartels (2005).

concentration of income and political power. Thomas Palley argues that the shifts toward corporate governance in which interests align more closely with financial markets has facilitated, and exacerbated, the destruction of union power.[18] The financial crisis itself may have been partly a result of politicians' responsiveness to those with money. Daron Acemoğlu and many other prominent economists have argued that excessive banking deregulation won from Congress and regulatory agencies by bank and financial lobbyists and their campaign contributions was a major contributor to the climate of reckless risk taking.[19] Other researchers have found a strong historical relationship between financial deregulation, bank failures, and inequality.[20]

Though some other advanced countries are plagued by similar problems, the U.S. political system appears particularly vulnerable to them. According to the International Institute for Democracy and Electoral Assistance, the United States, Chile, and New Zealand are the only three OECD countries that do not provide public funding for political parties. But New Zealand, like eleven other OECD countries but unlike the United States, has a statutory limit on how much parties can spend on campaigns.

Finally, it is worth highlighting the high cost of campaigning in the United States and the concomitant opportunities for money to affect outcomes. In 2010 the United States held midterm elections for 472 congressional seats, and the UK held elections for 650 constituencies in Parliament, which would decide executive as well as legislative power. In the United States, candidates and political parties spent about $3 billion on their campaigns, while

18. See Palley (2007). The BLS reports that union membership in the United States was 11.9 percent of the workforce in 2010, down from 20.1 percent in 1983 (U.S. Department of Labor, Bureau of Labor Statistics, "Union Members Summary," January 27, 2012).

19. Acemoğlu (2011).

20. Louis Story, "Income Inequality and Financial Crises," *New York Times*, August 21, 2010.

their UK counterparts spent a total of £57 million ($87 million).[21] This means that, as a share of GDP, the U.S. election cost roughly eight times as much as the UK election, and a staggering forty-seven times as much per seat.[22]

The oversize influence of the affluent is not always predictable of their support of one political party or a uniform point of view.[23] George Soros and Warren Buffett are clearly in favor of more redistributive government policies. Many wealthy individuals have championed progressive causes in the United States and around the world. The Gates Foundation is providing more support to poverty reduction worldwide than most governments. And grassroots mobilization campaigns to bring in a large number of small contributions in support of a political cause may aggregate to a large total and counteract the effects of a small number of very large donations. Nonetheless, it is only natural that those at the top use the means available to them in the political system to protect their share of income, even if many then give significant amounts to charitable causes. Increased income concentration at the top can thus lead to an inequality-reinforcing dynamic that both works through and affects the workings of the political system.

21. Electoral Commission (UK), "Election Expenditure," n.d. (www.electoral commission.org.uk/party-finance/party-finance-analysis/campaign-expenditure).

22. See www.opensecrets.org for more on election spending.

23. Dimock (2007).

6 WHAT CAN BE DONE?

IT IS BEYOND THE scope of this book to present detailed policy prescriptions to deal with the increase in inequality in the United States described in the preceding chapters.

Nevertheless we would like to outline the elements that should be considered to achieve greater balance in the distribution of income. They can usefully be grouped under three headings:

1. Policies that can affect *market incomes* (pre-tax and pre-transfer incomes) by affecting the underlying economic drivers of inequality.

2. Policies that affect *disposable real income* through taxes and transfers and reform of the so-called "tax expenditures."

3. *International cooperation* designed to close tax loopholes and reduce competition for lower taxes, which reduces the capacity of nation-states to pursue redistributive policies.

Market incomes are assumed to reflect productivity. Productivity is determined by skill and the amount and quality of capital available for labor to work with, as well as by a stable and predictable macro-economic and financial environment. There is a lot of evidence, however, that bargaining power and social norms also affect market incomes. Sky-high executive pay is considered more "normal" in the Unites States than, for example, in Japan, and unions were more able to affect wages when they were more powerful.

With respect to productivity, the most effective thing the United States can do both to impact the level and distribution of income and to enhance social mobility is to have an effective, inclusive, and equal opportunity–oriented system of education and skill formation. Given the extraordinarily high cost of health care in the United States and the wide disparities in insurance coverage, the provision of inclusive and effective health care is probably a close second, as only healthy citizens can generally be productive. The more unequal access to education and health care is, the more unequal market incomes are and the more likely it is that these disparities will become increasingly entrenched over time. But the skill and health of a citizen are not the only determinants of her salary. The amount of capital, including infrastructure, that this worker has access to is also an important driver of productivity. Efficient, stable, and inclusive capital markets that provide access to credit, at reasonable terms and in a way that is sustained and less subject to big shocks, are important for the distribution of income. Thus prudential regulation of the financial system is also essential. Good public transport infrastructure that serves all citizens and regions of a country is another factor that has a significant impact on the income distribution.

In addition, labor-market institutions and policies, including minimum wages and social norms, are necessary. Reality does not conform to the models of incomes determined in purely competitive markets, by productivity alone. There are many markets with indeterminacies due to monopolistic elements, and behavior is affected to a degree by historical and social norms. That is why a broader model of income determination, where bargaining and social norms play a role in wage setting, is more appropriate than the pure neoclassical competitive model. George Akerlof and Robert Shiller recognize this in their 2010 book, *Animal Spirits: How Human Psychology Drives the Economy, and Why*

It Matters for Global Capitalism. "However many articles there have been on fairness, and however important economists may consider fairness, it has been continually pushed into a back channel in economic thinking. . . . But fairness may be just as important as the economic motivations that are given prime time."[1] They also quote the great and very mainstream labor economist Albert Rees, who toward the end of his career recognized that social norms and perceptions of fairness are central in how remuneration is actually set in the real world.[2] The policy implication of this realization is that it is possible to affect income distribution by spreading the awareness of excessive pay at the top or subminimum wages at the bottom, thus shaping norms that put limits on excessive inequality. These norms can also be effectively promoted by legislation, for example, by means of regular adjustments to the minimum wage.

Market incomes can thus be affected by education, health, financial access, and infrastructure policies, as well as by measures such as regulations that promote social norms. The distribution of disposable income can of course be changed further through progressive taxation and by government expenditures that have a progressive impact. There is a huge ongoing debate on the nature of the tradeoff, if any, between efficiency and equity in this context. Opponents of progressive taxation argue that taxes discourage effort and investment and reduce productivity and that governments are inherently wasteful and inefficient in the use of the resources they collect through taxation. Proponents of progressive redistribution policies do not believe that reasonably high tax rates have a strong negative effect on incentives. And they do believe in the possibility of efficient provision of government services, which can be targeted to the poorer segments of the population. It is beyond the scope of this book to delve into this debate

1. See Akerlof and Shiller (2010).
2. Alerlof and Shiller (2010, p. 20).

in depth. We as authors do not necessarily agree among ourselves as to the optimal size of government services in an economy such as that of the United States. We are confident, however, that very large "win-win" outcomes can be achieved by fundamental tax reform and better targeting of the net benefits of public expenditures. One can debate whether the "optimal" marginal federal income tax rate on incomes above $500,000, or $1 million, should be 35, 39, or 42 percent, but it is difficult to justify people making millions of dollars a year paying a 15 percent federal income tax because their earnings predominately take the form of dividends and capital gains, or "carried interest" in private equity. There is little justification for the regressive nature of the Social Security tax, and little justification for mortgage interest tax credits on homes worth over a million dollars, about four times the value of the median house. There is no scientifically valid argument for rejecting a package that would tax carbon emissions at some modest rate and simultaneously reduce income taxes on lower incomes. There is no good argument against requiring the relatively wealthiest beneficiaries of Medicare to pay a greater share of its cost. If the negative effects of the very unequal distribution of income described in the preceding chapters are real, there are reasonable tax and expenditure reforms that would be considered both equitable and efficient remedies by a large majority of analysts who have examined these issues in great detail.

There is, finally, a third dimension to the policies that could be pursued. The global mobility of capital and high-skilled labor compared to that of less-skilled labor puts some constraints on the redistributive policies that a single nation, even one as large as the United States, can pursue. Having a high corporate tax rate, or high income tax rate, can create incentives for businesses and highly skilled people to move to places with lower taxes. While these incentive effects are sometimes exaggerated—taxes, after all, are only one factor that businesses or individuals consider when they choose their business or personal residence (and in any case,

American citizens are subject to U.S. tax no matter where they live)—they do exist, and greater globalization has increased their relevance. Many large corporations pay little corporate taxes to their "home countries": according to their accounting the profits were made elsewhere and are therefore not subject to the level of U.S. corporate tax rates "home" companies must pay. Though newspapers are full of stories about tax evasion in Greece and Italy these days, and the U.S. corporate income tax rate is one of the highest in the world, U.S. corporations actually pay fewer taxes as a share of GDP than those in Italy and Greece, according to the OECD, reflecting the possibility of cross-border shifts of profits as well as various domestic tax breaks. But cross-border tax evasion is just one of the many factors that result in poor incentives for revenue collection and are obstacles to carrying out redistributive policies. If public policies are to play the "balancing" and redistributive role vis-à-vis markets that they played in the twentieth century within nation-states, there is need for greater international cooperation and harmonization, not only in fighting against tax evasion and eliminating tax shelters but also in managing tax-related incentives in such a way that capital flight due to tax differentials is proactively discouraged.

7 CONCLUSION: NARROWING THE GAP

WE OPENED THIS VOLUME with Federal Reserve Chairman Ben Bernanke's reminder that equality of opportunity is a bedrock principle of American society. We feel that the reminder is apt because it is very much the way the country still sees itself and is also the way other nations see America. It is somewhat surprising, therefore, to recognize that the United States is not a very socially mobile nation and risks the further entrenchment of privilege because of education and health care systems that favor the relatively affluent and a political system where money can buy disproportionate influence on policy. Indeed, the discrepancy between traditional perceptions and the reality may be one reason that apparently unbridgeable political differences exist where compromise was once possible. It is very important, therefore, that the facts about inequality in the United States be available and accessible to interested citizens.

We have argued that tackling the worst effects of inequality and re-establishing a measure of equal opportunity requires increased investment in crucial public goods: first, education; second, a more progressive and simplified tax system; and third, increased international cooperation to avoid a race to the bottom. Education, tax, and other such policies are pursued by other high-performing advanced countries and can be shaped for the United States in a way that is fully consistent with an efficient and competitive American economy. The reforms needed are certainly not about stifling entrepreneurship, technology, or trade; indeed, we see all three as sources of prosperity and dynamism that should be nurtured and encouraged. But the side effects must be managed.

This three-pronged approach to reform is not original, but lack of originality does not make the suggested reforms any less worthwhile. It is easy to recognize that there is no greater inefficiency than wasting human potential and overlooking the promise of those who cannot afford adequate schools or the danger of falling ill. Citizens who fill the ranks of the long-term unemployed because of inadequate skills or the economy's inadequate aggregate demand represent a great burden to their society and to themselves. We must address the root causes of inequality so that a much better job can be done to ensure that opportunity is available to all and that rapid growth can be more sustainable.

REFERENCES

Acemoğlu, Daron. 2011. "Thoughts on Inequality and the Financial Crisis." Massachusetts Institute of Technology, January 7 (http://economics.mit.edu/files/6348).

———. 2002. "Technical Change, Inequality, and the Labor Market." *Journal of Economic Literature* 40, no. 1 (March): 7–72.

Akerlof, George, and Robert Shiller. 2010. *Animal Spirits: How Human Psychology Drives the Economy, and Why It Matters for Global Capitalism.* Princeton University Press.

Ali, Shimelse, and Uri Dadush. Forthcoming. "Where on Earth Is the Middle Class?" Washington: Carnegie Endowment for International Peace.

Alvaredo, Facundo, Tony Atkinson, Thomas Picketty, and Emmanual Saez. "The World Top Incomes Database." Paris: Paris School of Economics, Institute for New Economic Thinking, Center for Equitable Growth, Institute for New Economic Thinking at the Oxford Martin School (http://g-mond.parisschoolofeconomics.eu/topincomes).

Anderson, Sarah, Chuck Collins, Scott Klinger, and Sam Pizzigati. 2011. "Executive Excess 2011: The Massive CEO Rewards for Tax Dodging." Eighteenth Annual Executive Compensation Survey. Washington: Institute for Policy Studies, August (www.ips-dc.org/reports/executive_excess_2011_the_massive_ceo_rewards_for_tax_dodging).

Autor, David. 2010. "The Polarization of Job Opportunities in the U.S. Labor Market: Implications for Employment and Earnings." Paper prepared for Center for American Progress and the Hamilton Project. Washington: April (http://economics.mit.edu/files/5554).

Autor, David, Lawrence Katz, and Melissa Kearny. 2006. "The Polarization of the U.S. Labor Market." *American Economic Review Papers and Proceedings* 96, no. 2 (May): 189–95 (www.aeaweb.org/articles. php?doi=10.1257/000282806777212620).

Autor, David H., Frank Levy, and Richard J. Murnane. 2003. "The Skill Content of Recent Technological Change: An Empirical Exploration." *Quarterly Journal of Economics* 118, no. 4 (November): 1279–1333.

Baily, Martin Neil, and Robert Lawrence. 2004. "What Happened to the Great U.S. Job Machine? The Role of Trade and Electronic Offshoring." *Brookings Papers on Economic Activity*, no. 2: 211–84.

Bakija, Jon, Adam Cole, and Bradley T. Heim. 2010. "Jobs and Income Growth of Top Earners and the Causes of Changing Income Inequality: Evidence from U.S. Tax Return Data." Paper (www.indiana. edu/~spea/faculty/pdf/heim_JobsIncomeGrowthTopEarners.pdf).

Bartels, Larry M. 2005. "Economic Inequality and Political Representation." *American Journal of Political Science* 52, no. 1: 48–60.

Bernstein, Jared, Lawrence Mishel, and Heidi Shierholz. 2009. *State of Working America, 2008/2009*. Washington: Economic Policy Institute.

Bloom, Nicholas, Mirko Draca, and John Van Reenen. 2011. "Trade Induced Technical Change? The Impact of Chinese Imports on Innovation, IT and Productivity." NBER Working Paper 16717. Cambridge, Mass.: National Bureau of Economic Research.

Borjas, George J. 2003. "The Labor Demand Curve Is Downward Sloping: Reexamining the Impact of Immigration on the Labor Market." *Quarterly Journal of Economics* 118, no. 4: 1335–74.

Broda, Christian, and John Romalis. 2008. "Inequality and Prices: Does China Benefit the Poor in America?" Draft paper (www.etsg.org/ETSG2008/Papers/Romalis.pdf).

Brynjolfsson, Erik, and Andrew McAfee. 2011. *Race against the Machine: How the Digital Revolution Is Accelerating Innovation, Driving Productivity, and Irreversibly Transforming Employment in the Economy*. Lexington, Mass.: Digital Frontier Press.

Burtless, Gary. 1999. "Effects of Growing Wage Disparities and Changing Family Composition on the U.S. Income Distribution." Working Paper 4. Washington: Brookings, Center on Social and Economic Dynamics, July.

———. 2012. "Observations on Income Distribution Trends." Prepared for Seminar on Income Distribution, Brookings Institution, Washington, D.C., May 23.

Cancian, Maria, and Deborah Reed. 1998. "Assessing the Effects of Wives' Earnings on Family Income Inequality." *Review of Economics and Statistics* 80, no. 1 (February): 73–79.

Card, David. 2005. "Is the New Immigration Really So Bad?" *Economic Journal* 11, no. 506: F300–F323.

Card, David, Thomas Lemieux, and W. Craig Riddell. 2003. "Unionization and Wage Inequality: A Comparative Study of the U.S., the U.K., and Canada." NBER Working Paper 9473. Cambridge, Mass.: National Bureau of Economic Research, February.

Card, David, and John DiNardo. 2002. "Skill-Based Technological Change and Rising Wage Inequality: Some Problems and Puzzles." NBER Working Paper 8769. Cambridge, Mass.: National Bureau of Economic Research, February.

Carroll, Christopher C. 2000. "Why Do the Rich Save So Much?" In *Does Atlas Shrug? The Economic Consequences of Taxing the Rich*, edited by Joel B. Slemrod. Harvard University Press (www.econ2.jhu.edu/people/ccarroll/Why.pdf).

Cashell, Brian W. 2009. "The Fall and Rise of Household Savings." Paper prepared for the Congressional Research Service, no. 7-5700 (http://digitalcommons.ilr.cornell.edu/key_workplace/657).

Congressional Budget Office. 2011. "Trends in the Distribution of Household Income between 1979 and 2009." Publication 42729. Washington: Congressional Budget Office, October (http://cbo.gov/publication/42729).

Council of Economic Advisers. 1997. "Economic Report of the President." Washington: U.S. Government Printing Office, February (www.gpoaccess.gov/usbudget/fy98/pdf/erp.pdf).

Cowen, Tyler. 2011. "The Inequality That Matters." *American Interest* 6, no. 3 (January–February) (www.the-american-interest.com/article.cfm?piece=907).

Crotty, James. 2005. "The Neoliberal Paradox: The Impact of Destructive Product Market Competition and 'Modern' Financial Markets on Nonfinancial Corporation Performance in the Neoliberal Era." In *Financialization and the World Economy*, edited by Gerald Epstein. Northampton, Mass.: Edward Elgar.

———. 2009. "Structural Causes of the Global Financial Crisis: A Critical Assessment of the 'New Financial Architecture.'" *Cambridge Journal of Economics* 33, no. 4: 563–80.

Daly, Mary, and Robert Valletta. 2004. "Inequality and Poverty in the United States: The Effects of Rising Dispersion of Men's Earnings and

Changing Family Behavior." FRBSF Working Paper 2000-06. San Francisco: Federal Reserve Bank of San Francisco (www.frbsf.org/economics/economists/rvalletta/DV_Ineq-and-Pov_0719.pdf).

Dean, Judith, K. C. Fung, and Zhi Wang. 2007. "Measuring the Vertical Specialization in Chinese Trade." Office of Economics Working Paper 2007-01-A. Washington: U.S. International Trade Commission.

Dervis, Kemal. 2012. "The Inequality Trap." New York and Prague: Project Syndicate, March (http://beta.project-syndicate.org/commentary/the-inequality-trap).

Dimock, Michael. 2007. "Money Walks: Republicans Are Losing Ground among the Affluent, Too." Pew Research Center Publication. Washington: Pew Research Center, April (http://pewresearch.org/pubs/451/money-walks).

Dynan, Karen E., Jonathan Skinner, and Stephen Zeldes. 2004. "Do the Rich Save More?" *Journal of Political Economy* 112, no. 2: 397–444.

Fisher, Gordon. 1997. "The Development of the Orshansky Poverty Thresholds and Their Subsequent History as the Official U.S. Poverty Measure." Paper prepared for the U.S. Census Bureau. Washington: U.S. Census Bureau (www.census.gov/hhes/povmeas/publications/orshansky.html).

Frank, Robert H. 2011. *The Darwin Economy: Liberty, Competition and Good.* Princeton University Press.

Frank, Robert H., and Philip J. Cook. 1995. *The Winner-Take-All Society,* New York: Free Press.

Gilens, Martin. 2005. "Inequality and Democratic Responsiveness." *Public Opinion Quarterly* 69, no. 5, Special Issue: 778–96.

Goldin, Claudia, and Lawrence F. Katz. 2009. "Education and Technology: Supply, Demand and Income Inequality." *VOX,* June 9 (www.voxeu.org/index.php?q=node/3640).

Grossman, Gene, and Elhanan Helpman. 1995. "Technology and Trade." CEPR Discussion Papers. London: Center for Economic Policy Research, February.

Hacker, Jacob S., and Paul Pierson. 2010. *Winner-Take-All Politics.* New York: Simon & Schuster.

Hertz, Tom. 2006. "Understanding Mobility in America." Washington: Center for American Progress (www.americanprogress.org/issues/2006/04/Hertz_MobilityAnalysis.pdf).

Hirsch, Fred. 1977. *The Social Limits to Growth.* London: Routledge & Kegan Paul.

Isaacs, Julia, Isabel V. Sawhill, and Ron Haskins. 2008. *Getting Ahead or Losing Ground: Economic Mobility in America*. Washington: Brookings and Pew Charitable Trusts.

Kandel, William A. 2011. "The U.S. Foreign-Born Population: Trends and Selected Characteristics." CRS Report for Congress No. 7-5700. Washington: Congressional Research Service, January 18 (www.fas.org/sgp/crs/misc/R41592.pdf).

Kharas, Homi. 2010. "The Emerging Middle Class in Developing Countries." OECD Development Center Working Paper 25. Paris: OECD Publishing, January (www.oecd.org/dataoecd/12/52/44457738.pdf).

Krippner, Greta R. 2005. "The Financialization of the American Economy." *Socio-Economic Review* 3 (May): 173–208.

Krugman, Paul. 2008. "Trade and Wages, Reconsidered." *Brookings Papers on Economic Activity*, Spring, pp. 103–37.

———. 2009. *The Conscience of a Liberal*. New York: Norton.

Kumhof, Michael, and Romain Ranciere. 2010. "Inequality, Leverage and Crises." IMF Working Paper WP/10/68. Washington: International Monetary Fund.

———. 2011. "Unequal = Indebted." *Finance and Development* 48, no. 3 (September): 26–28.

Lee, David S. 1999. "Wage Inequality in the United States during the 1980s: Rising Dispersion or Falling Minimum Wage?" *Quarterly Journal of Economics* 114, no. 3 (August): 977–1023.

Levy, Frank, and Peter Temin. 2007. "Inequality and Institutions in 20th-Century America." NBER Working Paper 13106. Cambridge, Mass.: National Bureau of Economic Research, May (www.nber.org/papers/w13106.pdf).

Maki, Dean M., and Michael G. Palumbo. 2001. "Disentangling the Wealth Effect: A Cohort Analysis of Household Savings in the 1990's." Paper prepared for the Board of Governors of the Federal Reserve System. Washington: Federal Reserve (www.federalreserve.gov/pubs/feds/2001/200121/200121pap.pdf).

Milanovic, Branko. 2011. *The Haves and Have-nots: A Brief and Idiosyncratic History of Global Inequality*. New York: Basic Books.

———. 2009. "Income Inequality and Speculative Investment by the Rich and Poor in America Led to the Financial Meltdown." YaleGlobal Online (http://yaleglobal.yale.edu/content/two-views-global-crisis).

Miller, Erin. 2011. "Who Gives?" *The American Prospect*, December 19 (http://prospect.org/article/who-gives).

Minsky, Hyman. 1993. "The Financial Instability Hypothesis." In *The Handbook of Radical Political Economy*, edited by Philip Arestis and Malcolm Sawyer. Aldershot, UK: Edward Elgar (www.levyinstitute. org/pubs/wp74.pdf).

Organization for Economic Cooperation and Development. 2009. *PISA 2009 Technical Report*. Paris: OECD Publishing.

———. 2010. *Health Care Systems: Efficiency and Policy Settings*. Paris: OECD Library, November (www.oecd.org/document/39/0,33 43,en_2649_34587_46491431_1_1_1_1,00.html).

———. 2011a. "Growing Income Inequality in OECD Countries: What Drives It and How Can Policy Tackle It?" 2011. OECD Forum on Tackling Inequality. Paris: OECD (www.oecd.org/data oecd/32/20/47723414.pdf).

———. 2011b. "Divided We Stand: Why Inequality Keeps Rising." Paris: OECD, December (www.oecd.org/document/51/0,3746,en_ 2649_33933_49147827_1_1_1_1,00.html).

Ottaviano, Gianmarco I. P., and Giovanni Peri. 2006. "Rethinking the Effects of Immigration on Wages." NBER Working Paper 12497. Cambridge, Mass.: National Bureau of Economic Research, August.

Palley, Thomas. 2007. "Financialization: What it is and Why it Matters," Working Paper 525, Washington: Levy Institute (www.levy institute.org/pubs/wp_525.pdf).

Pencavel, John. 2006. "Earnings Inequality and Market Work in Husband-Wife Families." SCID Working Paper 289. Stanford University, Stanford Institute for Economic Policy Research.

Radelet, Steven, Dwight Perkins, Donald Snodgrass, Malcolm Gillis, and Michael Romer. 2001. *Economics of Development*. 5th ed. New York: Norton.

Rajan, Raghuram. 2010. *Fault Lines: How Hidden Fractures Still Threaten the World Economy*. Princeton University Press.

Rector, Robert, and Rachel Sheffield. 2011. "Air Conditioning, Cable TV, and an Xbox: What Is Poverty in the United States Today?" Backgrounder on Poverty and Inequality. Washington: Heritage Foundation (www.heritage.org/research/reports/2011/07/what-is-poverty).

Reich, Robert. 2010. *Aftershock: The Next Economy & America's Future*. New York: Random House.

Sachs, Jeffrey. 2011. *The Price of Civilization: Reawakening American Virtue and Prosperity*. New York: Random House.

Saint-Paul, Gilles. 2008. *Innovation and Inequality: How Does Technical Progress Affect Workers?* Princeton University Press.

Sawhill, Isabel. 2012. "Are We Headed toward a Permanently Divided Society?" Center on Children and Families Brief No. 48. March. Washington: Brookings Institution.

Short, Kathleen. 2011. "The Research: Supplemental Poverty Measure, 2010." *Current Population Reports.* Washington: U.S. Census Bureau, November.

Stepan, Alfred, and Juan Linz. 2011. "Comparative Perspectives on Inequality and the Quality of Democracy in the United States." *Perspectives on Politics* 9 (December): 841–56.

Stiglitz, Joseph E. 2010. *Freefall: America, Free Markets, and the Sinking of the World Economy.* London: Norton.

U.S. Bureau of Economic Analysis. "Annual Industry Accounts, Gross Domestic Product (GDP) by Industry" (www.bea.gov/industry/iedguide.htm#gpo).

U.S. Department of Labor, Bureau of Labor Statistics. 2012. *Occupational Outlook Handbook.* 2010–2011 edition. Washington: February 1 (www.bls.gov/oco/ocos154.htm).

U.S. Government Accountability Office. 2004. "International Trade: Current Government Data Provide Limited Insight into Offshoring of Services." Report to Congressional Requesters. GAO-04-932. September 2004 Washington: GAO, September (www.oecd.org/data oecd/3/32/35542215.pdf).

———. 2007. "Poverty in America: Economic Research Shows Adverse Impacts on Health Status and Other Social Conditions as Well as the Economic Growth Rate." Report to Congressional Requesters. GAO-07-344. Washington: GAO, January (www.gao.gov/new.items/d07344.pdf).

Western, Bruce, Deidre Bloome, and Christine Percheski. 2008. "Inequality among American Families with Children, 1975–2005." *American Sociological Review* 73 (December): 903–20.

Whalen, Charles J., and David A. Zalewski. 2010. "Financialization and Income Inequality: A Post-Keynesian Institutionalist Analysis." *Journal of Economic Issues* 34 (September): 757–78.

Wilkinson, Richard, and Kate Pickett. 2010. *The Spirit Level: Why More Equal Societies Almost Always Do Better.* Harmondsworth, UK: Penguin Books.

INDEX

BROOKINGS   The Brookings Institution is a private nonprofit organization devoted to research, education, and publication on important issues of domestic and foreign policy. Its principal purpose is to bring the highest quality independent research and analysis to bear on current and emerging policy problems. The Institution was founded on December 8, 1927, to merge the activities of the Institute for Government Research, founded in 1916, the Institute of Economics, founded in 1922, and the Robert Brookings Graduate School of Economics and Government, founded in 1924. Interpretations or conclusions in Brookings publications should be understood to be solely those of the authors.

Board of Trustees

John L. Thornton
  Chair
Strobe Talbott
  President
Robert J. Abernethy
Liaquat Ahamed
Dominic Barton
Robert M. Bass
Richard C. Blum
Crandall Bowles
Paul L. Cejas
Abby Joseph Cohen
Howard E. Cox
Alan M. Dachs
Steven A. Denning
Paul Desmarais Jr.
Cheryl Cohen Effron
Alfred B. Engelberg

Bart Friedman
Ann M. Fudge
Ellen Futter
Jeffrey W. Greenberg
Brian L. Greenspun
Glenn Hutchins
Shirley Ann Jackson
Benjamin R. Jacobs
Kenneth M. Jacobs
Suzanne Nora Johnson
Richard Kauffman
Richard A. Kimball Jr.
Nemir Kirdar
Klaus Kleinfeld
Philip H. Knight
Rajan Mittal
Nigel Morris
James Murran

Thomas C. Ramey
Edgar Rios
David M. Rubenstein
James S. Rubin
Haim Saban
Victoria P. Sant
Leonard D. Schaeffer
David F. Swensen
Lynn Thoman
Larry D. Thompson
Michael L. Tipsord
Andrew H. Tisch
Antoine W. van Agtmael
John W. Wilhelm
Tracy R. Wolstencroft
Daniel Yergin
Daniel B. Zwirn

Honorary Trustees

Elizabeth E. Bailey
Zoë Baird Budinger
Rex J. Bates
Alan R. Batkin
Geoffrey T. Boisi
Louis W. Cabot
James W. Cicconi
William T. Coleman Jr.
Arthur B. Culvahouse Jr.
Kenneth W. Dam
Vishakha N. Desai
Mario Draghi
Kenneth M. Duberstein
Lawrence K. Fish

Cyrus F. Freidheim Jr.
David Friend
Lee H. Hamilton
William A. Haseltine
Teresa Heinz
F. Warren Hellman
Joel Z. Hyatt
James A. Johnson
Ann Dibble Jordan
Vernon E. Jordan Jr.
Herbert M. Kaplan
Breene M. Kerr
Donald F. McHenry
Arjay Miller

Mario M. Morino
Maconda Brown O'Connor
William A. Owens
Frank H. Pearl
Charles W. Robinson
James D. Robinson III
Warren B. Rudman
B. Francis Saul II
Ralph S. Saul
Michael P. Schulhof
John C. Whitehead
Stephen M. Wolf
Ezra K. Zilkha

ASHLAND COMMUNITY & TECHNICAL COLLEGE

3 3631 1137210 7

HC 110 .I5 I524 2012

WITHDRAWN

Inequality in America

CPSIA information can be obtained at www.ICGtesting.com
Printed in the USA
BVOW080743150213

313327BV00001B/3/P

9 780815 724216